# Life Here and Hereafter

# Life Here and Hereafter

## Swami Rama

www.HimalayanInstitute.in

Himalayan Institute India
Near Nageshwar Mandir
Chatnag, Jhunsi
Allahabad – 211019 (U.P.)
Phone: +91 7408434140

Email: info@HimalayanInstitute.in
Web: www.HimalayanInstitute.in



ISBN-13: 9780893890025

Printed in India, 2016

Cover design by Stephanie Lora

# CONTENTS

# *Foreword*

*Life Here and Hereafter* is drawn from the lectures given by Sri Swami Rama during one of his world tours. Students and staff of Risso University in Japan, the University of Hawaii, the Unity Churches, and the Menninger Foundation in the United States were only some of the audiences that heard this teacher from the Himalayas.

While it is difficult to represent the insightful spontaneity provoked during the tour, the reader possesses, nevertheless, an advantage unavailable to the former audiences. For these pages retain the nectar of those lectures but in a distilled and cohesive presentation. The liberties of Swamiji's extemporaneous speech have been transformed into the clarity of his written form, in this way reaching the ever-widening circle of aspirants, to quench their spiritual thirst.

The inspiration of these lectures came from that portion of ancient wisdom called the Upanishads. One of these scriptures, the *Kathopanishad,* describes a perennial mystery that most people are fearful to face: the enigma of death. A story unfolds into a dialogue between Yama, the King of Death, and Nachiketa, the young seeker of Death's meaning. The characterization has a universal quality. For the inevitability of this dreadful mystery finally overtakes even the most courageous. Who can withstand Death?

The resolution of Death and his fearful presence remains the challenge of these pages.

Justin O'Brien, DTh

## CHAPTER 1

# *The Value of the Upanishads*

The Vedas are universally recognized as the earliest spiritual revelations in the history of mankind. They are four in number—*Rig, Sama, Yajur,* and *Atharva—and* are divided into sections that apply to the different clans of ancient society. The real aim and object of the various clans was to perform the religious rites and sacrifices *(yajnas)* appropriate to them. As the nature of the oblations and the mantras connected with them differed from one clan or community to another, each group adopted and developed the injunctions and tests suitable to itself. These differences are reflected in the content of the Vedas and in the grammar for learning and explaining the mantras. Each Veda contains different Upanishads, all of which are accepted as authoritative revelation by the traditional systems of India. Many savants have made Upanishadic commentaries, and they are all regarded as highly valuable by modern scholars.

The Vedas contain mantras or inspired hymns uttered by the great *rishis (sages)* of Truth. Vyasa collected the scattered gems of these Vedic truths and divided them into four sections. The oldest of them is the *Rig Veda*. The rishis used to sing these hymns using a musical scale with seven notes to an octave.

It is pertinent to mention here that the seven notes of an octave in music were first discovered in ancient India by the rishis. Also, the seven spheres in the universe were understood by the yogis long before the modern world knew of them. Today many scientists believe that even the electrons of the atom are in seven spheres. An atom is made of electrons, neutrons, and protons. Neutrons constitute the central nucleus and govern the whole mass of the atom. The electrons move around the nucleus in different orbits, which are associated with different amounts of energy. The higher the electron orbit, the more energy there is associated with it. Similarly, in our bodies the *Atman* (Self) is centrally situated, and the seven chakras are the orbits associated with the different amounts of energy. The higher the position of the chakra, the more energy there is associated with it. This phenomenon was discovered by Indian yogis ages before its rediscovery by modern science.

The Upanishads generally form part of the *Aranyakas,* which are themselves a part of the *Brahmana* portion of the Vedas, though some of them form part of the *Samhita* portion as well. The Upanishads comprise the *jnanakand,* or "knowledge portion," as opposed to the ritualistic portion of the Vedas, which is known as the *karmakand,* or "work portion." They are also known as the *Vedanta,* "the end of the Vedas," as they generally form the last part of the Vedas and express the highest purpose of the Vedas with respect to the supreme knowledge that frees the individual soul from bondage.

The term *Upanishad* has been interpreted variously by scholars. "The Western scholars," says Professor Max Muller, "are agreed on deriving Upa-ni-shad from the root *sad,* to sit down, preceded by two prepositions, *ni,* down, and *upa,* near, so that it expresses the idea of session, an assembly of pupils, sitting down near the teacher to listen to his instructions." He himself also holds this view, though he admits that the word never occurs in this specific sense anywhere in the ancient literature. According to the Eastern commentators, the word *Upanishad* comes from the Sanskrit word *sad,* which means (1) to destroy, (2) to guide, and (3) to loosen. If we take the first meaning, we find that an Upanishad is "that which destroys the ignorance and the superstition of the individual soul." If we adopt the second sense, the meaning of the word would be "that which guides the individual soul toward the attainment of the final goal." The third meaning signifies "that which loosens the attachment of our material body to earthly conditions and to the material world." As the light of the sun dispels darkness, so the light of the Upanishads destroys the darkness of our ignorance.

The term *Upanishad* thus means "that which destroys the ignorance of the individual soul; that which guides the seeker toward the attainment of the highest wisdom and perfection; that which loosens our attachment to the material world, to earthly attractions, and to our own physical, perishable self."

Shankara and other commentators have interpreted the Upanishads in these three ways:

I. The Upanishads are recognized as the revelations vouchsafed to the Vedic seers while they were in the most purifed and transcendental state *(samadhi)*. They imparted these truths to their disciples, who in turn ensured their preservation by transmitting them orally from generation to generation.

2. The Upanishads teach the universal and eternal truth. This truth is one without a second. The Vedic seers have expressed this truth, as they saw it in their moments of revelation, through the vehicle of words, which are called *mantras*. The word *mantra* means "that which liberates the mind from grief and sorrow."

3. The Vedic scriptures declare that Brahman became "many" to realize its own glory and greatness. This multiplicity or plurality is but a transformation assumed by the Absolute, which in its totality remains one without a second. Ignorant men make themselves mere toys in the hands of diversity. They go through this world of contingencies and delusions without gaining anything worth having. They create for themselves an eternal cycle of births and deaths, from which they are unable to escape. The teachings of the Upanishads show the path of liberation from this cycle of births and deaths.

Of the several commentators of the Upanishads, the most towering is Acharya Shankara, who was a penetrating thinker and yogi, perhaps the greatest metaphysician the world has ever seen. He made commentaries on the twelve principal Upanishads that are considered the oldest and the most authentic. There are other Upanishads also, which make up the rationalistic portion of the Vedas.

The Upanishads are not treatises written by scholars on any particular subject. They are the repositories of that wisdom which is eternal and uncreated by human agencies. We find in them the great truths of life here and hereafter, as also the ideals of earthly existence. Shankara calls them the *Moksha Shastra* (Liberation Scriptures) or *Brahma Vidya* (Knowledge of Brahman) because the Upanishads reveal the knowledge of the highest Absolute, Brahman. Those who are genuine seekers of this truth and have purifed their hearts by transforming them into pure consciousness can cut the knots of the cycle of births and deaths and attain liberation. The subject matter of the Upanishads is Self-realization, which brings about the utter extinction of the fire of worldly desires and the simultaneous attainment of supramental knowledge.

According to the great sage Yati Sadananda, the name *Upanishad* denotes Vedanta. He says that the gems of the Vedanta philosophy have been gathered from the Upanishads. The Upanishads are like the grapes, while Brahma Vidya or Vedanta philosophy is the juice squeezed out of them. Vedanta is a rational and logical philosophy that has systematized for all times the universal truths adumbrated by the Vedic seers.

CHAPTER 2

# *The* Kathopanishad: *Its Place in Upanishadic Literature*

The *Kathopanishad* belongs to the *Katha Shakha* of the *Krishna Yajurveda*. The rationalistic portion of the *Yajurveda* contains a few important Upanishads, of which the *Kathopanishad* is the most precious. This Upanishad consists of two main chapters, each comprising three cantos or dialogues. The first chapter consists of seventy-one mantras, and the second chapter consists of forty-eight mantras.

The *Kathopanishad* is primarily a metaphysical work envisaging the highest philosophical truth in poetic manner; thus it became one of the chief sources from which the later Bhagavad Gita freely borrows. As a matter of fact, mantras 1, 2, 15, 18, and 19 from the *Kathopanishad* have been placed more or less literally into the Bhagavad Gita (VIII.11, II.20, and II.19, respectively). The conception of a cosmic tree in the Bhagavad Gita (XV) and the supremacy of the Atman over the ascending gradations of the senses, their objects, the mind, and intellect (III.42-43) likewise appear to have been directly inspired from the *Kathopanishad* (II.3.1 and I.3,10-11).

Two of the most impressive features of the *Kathopanishad* are the beautiful allegory of the "chariot of the body" and the death and dream approaches to the problem of reality. The whole of the *Kathopanishad* is charged with lofty metaphysical speculations about the immortality of the soul and contains practical suggestions for the attainment of Atman. The main theme of the

*Kathopanishad* is the transcendental immanence of one non-dual reality, to realize which the mundane impediments of life here in this world have to be transcended. According to somc interpreters, the *Kathopanishad* has its natural termination at the end of the first chapter, as suggested by the formal repetition of words and the *phalasruti* (statement of results) that appear at its conclusion. The second chapter seems to have been tacked on to the original redaction of the Upanishad—thus signifying two strata of composition. But ancient and reliable interpreters still take the entire *Kathopanishad* to be one unit.

The *Kathopanishad* expounds the mystery of life and death. It elucidates the law of karma and the destiny of all beings, and points out the way to gain perfect liberation from grief and distress. This Upanishad is concerned with something quite uncommon, beginning with an instructive story depicting how each person possesses a host of doubts as well as an abundance of faith, and ultimately hankers after the highest knowledge and happiness. Here the young seeker, Nachiketa, personifies the universal questioner, and unique answers are given by the King of Death himself. Those who are already traversing the path of contemplation and self-realization will easily understand the theme of this beautiful story. Nachiketa and the King of Death may be compared respectively to the lower mind and to the highest discriminating intelligence of the individual, in the same manner as Arjuna and Sri Krishna have been interpreted in the Gita.

Naturally enough, all seekers after truth are riddled with doubts, and so they argue like atheists in order to arrive at a solution to their problems and to find a genuine proof of the final truth. Nachiketa is the symbol of the sincere inquisitive seeker after truth. The self-realized master, the King of Death, tests the intense craving of Nachiketa. He tempts Nachiketa in various ways with offers of pleasure and wealth, but Nachiketa is not moved. Eventually Nachiketa is granted the cherished grace of God-realization. After drinking the nectar of immortality, Nachiketa obtains absolute freedom from worldly fetters, thus setting a shining example for all seekers after truth.

The beautiful story of Nachiketa teaches us that he who renounces everything for the sake of self-realization, and who is intensely sincere, is sure to obtain the highest fruits of yoga. All the pleasures, the highest joys that one experiences in life, do not continue for long, and one cannot extend their duration indefinitely. The greatest pleasures of this earth are but transitory. Pleasure and pain are conditioned by our thoughts and deeds on this earth. One cannot change them, no matter where one goes. If a man goes into a wilderness and leads a lonely life, he finds that his desires drive him crazy because he cannot throw away his mind. And as long as he has not discarded his mind in this life, how can he expect that after death he will get rid of all his desires? He who wants to divest himself of his desires will have to begin here in this life, and by attaining self-control, rise above earthly desires. For all worldly desires simply drag him back to this worldly plane. They cannot help him to get out of it. Any slackening, therefore, of our attachment to the material body and material conditions is of immeasurably more value than all the wealth and comforts that can be had on this plane.

**The Story**

The wisdom explained through the story of Nachiketa is considered the highest by seekers of truth. It is the wisdom of the eternal Self, the knowledge of our own being. True being is beyond the reach of our senses. How we can acquire that highest bliss is therefore a question that rises uppermost in the minds of all seekers after truth. This most vital problem has been dealt with in the *Kathopanishad*. The story tells us how a young man attained the highest wisdom by going to the abode of Yam a, the Ruler of Death. The story of the *Kathopanishad* has three characters:

Vajasravas, Nachiketa, and Yama. Yama was the first man who died, thus becoming the ruler of all departed souls. Vajasravas was a wealthy man who once performed a sacrifice called *Vishvajita,* which required that he should give up all his possessions and pleasures and distribute everything he had to the great seers and learned Brahmins. This sacrifice was considered one of the greatest sacrifices of those days. To anyone who is ready to sacrifice his immediate gains in the faith that all transitory things should be sacrificed for a larger and lasting end, to him comes the knowledge of reality.

Vajasravas had a son named Nachiketa. He was a young boy, but he had tremendous faith and he was a seeker after truth. Vajasravas, although he promised to distribute his wealth and possessions, did not do it as satisfactorily as the wise men assembled there had expected him to. He gave them only those cows that were old, dry, blind and diseased, those that were practically of little or no use to anybody. He kept the good ones for himself.

Nachiketa, realizing the nature of the sacrifice and overwhelmed with *shraddha* (faith), was grieved and hurt. He went straight to his father and asked him, "Father, to whom will you give me?" Vajasravas did not answer. When the boy repeated the same question twice and thrice, he got extremely angry and said, "You I shall give to the Ruler of Death (Yama)."

The young boy, believing that his father had actually meant what he said, began to prepare himself to go to the abode of Yama. He was happy to obey the command of his father and comforted himself with the thought that he would be the first person to go alive to the abode of Death. His heart was pure and he was very eager to obey the order of his father and to unravel the mystery of earthly life and its gains.

It may be mentioned here that an aspirant who is prepared to be initiated even by Death will surely achieve the higher knowledge. The student of yoga will realize that after his renunciation of worldly desires he becomes immortal, even if he dies from the worldly point of view. Going to the abode of Death means attaining fearlessness. One who is prepared to die for the sake of higher knowledge will not find the Ruler of Death at home when one goes to the latter's abode. Every aspirant should achieve this state of mind before treading the path of contemplation and self-realization. Nachiketa said, "There is nothing in death. All beings flourish like grain and die again. Now I shall be the first one to discover truth and reveal the mystery of death."

**The Three Boons**

When Nachiketa entered the realm of death, the king of Death was away from home. Nachiketa waited for three days without food and water at the abode of Death, and there was none there to attend on him. (Here one is reminded of *sanyasa diksha,* the initiation onto the path of renunciation. When *sanyasa diksha* is given, the disciple is examined in several ways. For example, he is kept two or three days in a lonely burial ground in order to test his fearlessness). But Nachiketa remained there undaunted because he was virtuous and was possessed of an unwavering faith and determination. On returning home the King of Death saw the young aspirant and was sorry that he had not been shown proper hospitality. There is a belief that if a guest goes away without receiving due hospitality, he leaves all the bad luck with the householder and takes away all the virtues from the latter. All the good actions cease to produce beneficial results in the home where the guests are not given due hospitality.

The King of Death said, "0 Brahmin, my salutations to thee. As you have stayed in my house for three days and three nights without receiving any hospitality, you may ask three boons, and I shall grant you whatever you wish to obtain. I am extremely pleased to grant you good luck and good fortune."

Young Nachiketa answered, "The first boon that I ask is this: grant that my father who was so angry with me will not worry about me. 0 King, grant him all blessings and happiness of the world." Imagine the filial piety of the son asking as the first favor that his father be pleased with him! The Ruler of Death granted that wish with the greatest pleasure and said, "0 Nachiketa, your father will happily recognize you and treat you with the greatest love and kindness."

Nachiketa said, "In heaven there is neither fear nor death, neither age nor decay, neither hunger nor thirst, neither pain nor suffering. There is perpetual bliss. Ruler of Death, you alone know how, by performing sacrifice, mortals can attain this blissful heaven. This is my second boon that I ask. I want to know the nature of the sacrifice that leads a mortal to heaven." The Ruler of Death granted his second request, and revealed the mysteries of the sacrifice by which mortals can dwell in heaven. Nachiketa was a very bright student. After learning the sacrifice from the King of Death, he repeated it so successfully that the King of Death, being well pleased, gave him a supplementary blessing. To reward him for his proficiency, the King of Death called that fire-sacrifice after Nachiketa's name *(Nachiketagni)* and presented him with a many-colored chain as an ornament.

After this, the King of Death asked Nachiketa to choose the third boon, and what Nachiketa asked was this: "There is a belief that after a man departs from the world he is gone forever. There are others who believe that he is born again, that even after death man does not die in the real sense but remains on a subtle plane with his subtle body, that only the outer physical garment is thrown away and that is called death. Some believe that one who dies, lives. Which of these is true? What exists after death? Explain it to me. This is my third request—the truth relating to the mystery of death."

**Price of the Last Boon**

The Ruler of Death did not want to explain the mystery of death to Nachiketa without testing the intense eagerness of his disciple. He said, "0 Nachiketa, even the *devas* (gods) have doubts about this question. It is very difficult for anyone to understand. Ask any other boon and I shall grant it to you with great pleasure."

Nachiketa replied, "When the devas themselves do not understand this mystery, and there is none wiser than yourself to give an answer, 0 King of Death, I shall not make any other request. There is no other boon equal to this and I must know the secret. "

The Ruler of Death tempted Nachiketa by promising to give him a long span of life, lasting for hundreds of years, with all the pleasures available in heaven. He said that he would grant him children, grandchildren, and great-grandchildren, fine horses and elephants, gold, jewels and rare gems, and the kingdom of the earth to rule. But he said that he did not want to grant the third boon. Yama, the King of Death said, "I shall fulfill all your desires except this, for it is the greatest secret of life. All these damsels in the celestial regions, such damsels as cannot be had by ordinary mortals, they shall be yours if you want them. But do not ask me that question again. I do not wish to divulge the secret of life and death."

But young Nachiketa would not be lured by these fascinating temptations. He said, "What shall I do with all these transitory and perishable objects? Everything that is perceived by the senses is momentary, and life on this plane is subject to change by death and decay. Even life in heaven is not worth living without acquiring the knowledge of liberation. All your dancing damsels and worldly attractions are merely sensual pleasures. 0 King of Death, keep them with you. No one can acquire happiness by worldly wealth. All the material enjoyments of this world, and even heavenly life, are subject to change. After knowing the perishability of this world, who will long for mere longevity? I don't care to live for a thousand years. What shall I do with such a long life if I cannot acquire the highest wisdom and attain the highest knowledge?" Finally, Nachiketa repeated, "When there is doubt even among the devas and when even they do not know the answer to this question, it is you alone who can reveal the mystery, and that is my third boon."

Nachiketa would not accept any gift other than the knowledge about the secret of death. The young seeker after truth went to the abode of the Ruler of Death to acquire the highest knowledge. This story should be of immense value to the true and sincere aspirants. Those who attain the highest knowledge and immortality by reaching the state of consciousness, they alone can unravel the mystery of death and explain it to those treading the path of yoga. The mystery of life after death is revealed only to those who are not tempted by the charms and temptations of life on this plane; to them the Ruler of Death will reveal the secret of the mystery of death.

CHAPTER 3

# *Imperatives for Spiritual Aspirants*

In ancient India the highest spiritual knowledge was imparted only to earnest aspirants who were possessed of self-restraint and high moral discipline. It was given only to those people who were free from the desire for enjoyments that are attainable by the performance of rites, sacrifices, and so forth. According to Shankara, the architect of Advaita philosophy, such aspirants must possess the preliminary moral disciplines collectively known as *sadhana chatustaya*. This presupposes the ability to distinguish between eternal and purely ephemeral values *(nityanitya vastu vivekah),* the complete giving up of the last trace of desire to enjoy the pleasures of the senses both in this world and the world to come *(ihamutra artha bhoga viragah),* the cultivation of virtues such as restraint of body and mind *(sama-damadi-sadhana-sampat),* and a burning desire to liberate oneself from the bondage of finite existence *(mumuksutva).* The acquisition of these qualifications was considered indispensable for entering on the further course of discipline consisting of the hearing of the sacred texts from a competent guru *(shravana),* contemplation on their importance by employing all one's power of reasoning *(manana),* and unremitting meditation on the ultimate truth enshrined in them *(nididhyasana).*

That is why it has been customary for a spiritual teacher to test the sincerity and earnestness of the pupil before revealing the knowledge to him, because spiritual pursuit is a serious undertaking. Mere curiosity is not sufficient to tread the path of higher life. Deep sincerity and staunch faith are very important. Such earnest seekers are very rare indeed, and therefore spiritual teachers always test the sincerity of their pupils in several ways. The King of Death, assuming his role as a spiritual master, did not grant the third boon immediately, but put the sincerity of Nachiketa to test.

According to the story of the *Kathopanishad,* the truth relating to rebirth rests with rare teachers like Yama, the King of Death. In order to know this mystery, the aspirant should faithfully tread the path described by the *Kathopanishad* and should not be led astray by any of the temptations that may be offered to him. Even the unrivalled joys of heaven and the greatest pleasure of this world should not ensnare him. One who is determined like Nachiketa shall some day achieve his goal. Worldly pleasures are ephemeral by nature. Even a long life span of hundreds of years is not to be desired so long as death is sure to occur in the end.

According to the religion one professes, such are the fruits one gets after death. For example, the Muslims believe that in heaven there are plenty of watersheds, fruits, beautiful damsels, music and dancing, and so on. There are certain sects who believe in a heaven of heroes where battles are fought against their enemies and against ferocious animals. All these heavens are nothing but mental realms where man's highest desires are allegedly fulfilled.

All human beings seek certain desires they consider as the most delectable, and then they wish for a realm where such desires could possibly be fulfilled. Therefore, the longing for a heaven projects a realm that is a replica of the heaven one sought to achieve. Thus a heaven is but a projection of our own ideas and desires that are no more real than our dreams. They seem real because they are of our world of thoughts. We are the makers of this world because we are the thinkers. If we build an imaginary castle, that castle looks real so long as that pleasure of thought persists, even as a dream is real so long as it lasts. The image that lasts for a certain duration under certain conditions seems real till it ends. When a man goes into a sound dreamless state of sleep, the whole world will vanish in relation to him and he will not be conscious of any phenomena around him. All the persons and possessions to which one is attached vanish in the state of deep sleep.

Thus even dreams are realities, and the realms of heaven are realities, under certain conditions. When a man dreams, he is in heaven till he wakes up, but then the reality of the dream vanishes and other ideas rush in. This world is like a dream, and we will realize it is so when we shut the doors of our senses. As each face is different from all others, so each mind and each perception is different from all others. No one can see things precisely as the other sees. We may see similar things, but not the same things.

Life flies by quickly. We should seek the highest and realize that which is permanent. It is common experience that a prolonged pleasure results in monotony, with all its attendant consequences of depression, pain, and so on. A pleasure which is to be enjoyed needs, therefore, to be fleeting. We do not wish the same sensual pleasures to continue forever. Everything is relative, depending upon comparison. Pleasure depends upon comparison. And since comparison is the measure of enjoyment, how can one be sure that the same happiness is worth having in some other realm? Will it not also be like a dream unless one wakes up and goes further up?

If we ask any ordinary man whether he would prefer the knowledge of the mystery of death to earthly pleasures, his answer would invariably be in the negative. Nachiketa, however, refused to accept the transitory pleasures offered by the King of Death, and insisted that he must know the mystery of death and nothing else. The question concerning the mystery of death was most vital for him. Nachiketa asked: "0 King of Death, reveal that vital truth which even angels and devas have doubted. I do not want any other boon than this."

The King of Death was extremely pleased with the sincerity of young Nachiketa. He could not dissuade him from his firm resolve to unveil the mystery of death. Anyone who wants to tread the path of yoga should have this unshakable determination to succeed like Nachiketa. Anyone having a similar determination to reach the final goal will succeed in the end. Firmness of character is very essential. Curiosity-mongers should keep away from this path. One who has never-failing faith struggles on and on until the goal is reached.

The aspirant, first, should be firm like Nachiketa; second, temptations should not drag him to the sense plane or to the pleasures of life; third, he must hold before his eyes the ideal of the young seeker Nachiketa, who despised everything and cared for nothing, not even the highest pleasures of heaven.

## CHAPTER 4

# *The Good and the Pleasant*

Having tested the disciple and found him fit for knowledge, the King of Death said, "There are two things in this world. The one is good *(shreya)* and the other is pleasant *(preya)*. And these two change the souls of human beings in various ways. The wise accept that which is good, the ignorant resort to that which is pleasant." In the plane on which we live today there are two courses of action. One, though difficult, leads to the knowledge of the highest truth; the other, though apparently very pleasant, is but ephemeral. One who pursues what is pleasant misses the highest truth, and one who treads the path of good misses what is pleasant. The two paths are mutually exclusive and opposed to each other. The acceptance of the one implies the rejection of the other.

This very implication of two paths is conveyed also by the terms *higher (para)* knowledge and *lower (apara)* knowledge, referred to in the *Mundaka Upanishad* as well as in the *Ishavasyam (Isha) Upanishad* as "the path of knowledge" *(vidya)* and "the path of the world" *(avidya)*. The same typical distinction between the two paths is also brought out in the conversation between Narada and Sanatkumara in the *Chandogya Upanishad* (VII. 1.23), where the higher knowledge of the Self has been put on a very high pedestal.

The words *good* and *pleasant* used in the *Kathopanishad* signify two opposite tendencies leading to two different paths. Here the word *good* means "the highest good; illumination;

liberation." *Pleasant* means "sense pleasures (enjoyed through wealth, wife, children, and other material objects)." The two come to all persons, and one is free to choose between them. Choosing is inevitable because it is not ordinarily possible to adopt both paths simultaneously. If one is following the pleasant, it cannot be possible to follow the good. The choice is free—but the results of the choice are binding. To many people the good and the pleasant present themselves as a mixture, but like an ant sifting sugar from the mixture of sugar and sand, the wise person discriminates between the two and prefers the good to the pleasant. The unwise person, however, chooses the pleasant out of greed and avarice. The same idea is echoed in the immortal words of Jesus Christ: "No man can serve two masters: for either he will hate the one and love the other; or else he will hold to the one, and despise the other. Ye cannot serve God and mammon" (Matt. 6:24). Mammon is the pleasant and God is the good. One has to make a choice between the two according to one's inner evolution. The one who chooses the good understands very clearly what Christ meant when he said, "Lay not up for yourselves treasures upon earth, where moth and rust doth corrupt, and where thieves break through and steal: But lay up for yourselves treasures in heaven, where neither moth nor rust doth corrupt, and where thieves do not break through nor steal" (Matt. 6: 19-20).

These very two paths are signified by the Sanskrit words *pravritti* and *nivritti* (both derived from the parent word *vritti,* but with differing prefixes) and denote two entirely different attitudes or tendencies of mind *(manas)* and mind-stuff *(chitta). Vritti* literally means "whirlpool," connoting the circling of thought waves of the mind and mind-stuff. The mind, the determinative faculty *(buddhi),* the mind-stuff, and egoism *(ahankara)* form the group called the "internal instrument" *(antahkarana)* of the human body. They are but various processes in the mind-stuff, which, through cognition and action and reaction of sensations in the cerebral centers, affect the nature of thoughts and mold the subconscious *(samskara)* and conscious life of an individual.

Thoughts not only determine the quality of our actions and

our future reincarnations, but they also give us the power to act. A person is like a tethered animal, tied to his samskara (subconscious life) as though to a post or pole. Thought is the main material source in the human body, in which all the various faculties of human beings find their origin. Thoughts being the most dominant force in the human organism, a person's inner evolution is basically dependent on their quality. Not only one's psychology but even one's physiology is very much affected by one's own thoughts. And that is why these two Sanskrit terms, pravritti and nivritti, emphasizing the importance of vrittis, carry within them a deep knowledge of man's psychophysical nature. It was as a result of deep probing by the ancient rishis that they gave predominant importance to thought in humankind's spiritual evolution. "Let noble thoughts come to us from every side"(A *no bhadra kratavo vantu vishvatah)* was the prayer of the rishis in the *Rig Veda* (I.89.1). "Let that Almighty confer on us a pure intellect" *(Sa no budhya shubhaya samyunaktu)* was the call of the rishi in the *Shvetashvatara Upanishad* (III.4). The famous *gayatri* mantra prays to the Almighty to enlighten our intellect *(dhiyo yo nah prachodayat)*. It has been the sages' eternal contribution to the future of humanity to direct their prayers for the attainment of pure intellect and noble thoughts. This very depth of knowledge about the psychophysiological nature of the human organism inspired Patanjali to define yoga as the restraint and control of the thought waves of the mind-stuff and to prescribe techniques for the same in his famous Yoga Sutras.

Now let us return to the two Sanskrit terms. With the prefix *pra* added to *vritti,* it becomes *pravritti,* which means "circling forward" or "revolving outward" toward mundane things, with a view to appropriating or accumulating them for the selfish ends of the empirical self. On the other hand, with the prefix *ni* added to *vritti,* it becomes *nivritti,* which means "circling or revolving inward" away from things and concentrating solely on the true Self. Thus *pravritti* stands for worldly enjoyment and *nivritti* stands for renunciation of worldly desires. Nivritti implies the pursuit of the good. The first represents the "me and mine," the second stands for "not I but Thou." Excess of pravritti tends to make a person a demon, while excess of nivritti leads him to the divine. For the common man or woman, however, a judicious balance has got to be struck, for which a pure intellect is an indispensable concomitant. Nachiketa was not one of the common lot, for he declined forthright all the earthly pleasures and temptations offered to him by the King of Death, whereby eventually he was entitled to receive the highest knowledge.

The wise seers, after long discrimination, discovered that the path leading to the pleasures of life is not permanent. On this material plane we do not find any pleasure which is not attended with its opposite (pain or suffering) in some form or other. The ancient seers followed the path that kept them away from pleasure and pain alike. They pursued that goodness which brings in its train perpetual happiness. This happiness is absolutely independent; it does not depend upon anything worldly or heavenly. True happiness does not depend on the senses and their concomitants. Therefore, it is evident that wise people prefer the good path to the pleasant path. One who is free from desires is also free from the constant running after wealth, name, and fame, and is always free. One who hankers after the glamours of the world and forgets his real object in life falls prey to the wiles of the world.

The ordinary person follows the pleasant path, propelled by his native desires and tendencies; but the wise sage follows the path that leads to absolute goodness. One who chooses the path of pleasure and who is ruled by ambition and greed dwells in the darkness of ignorance. That which does not lead the aspirant to the knowledge of the Self seems to be attractive. Sense objects, however, can never give the aspirant anything permanent; no real happiness can be had within the realm of the senses. The subject matter of the *Kathopanishad* again and again relates to the discrimination between what is pleasant and what is good.

The King of Death said, "0 Nachiketa, you have renounced all that is pleasant. You have not cared for the pleasures of this plane, nor those of heaven. You have renounced the path which is followed by the majority of the people, the path of delusion and death."

Most people follow the path of pleasure, which keeps them in darkness about the real nature of the true Self. They never pay attention to its real nature. They never pay attention to the real side of life and believe only in the transitory pleasures of the world. But a fortunate few among them wake up frightened and disgusted with life. There is a craving inherent in each soul for something higher and permanent. In spite of being deluded, our souls experience an innate craving that, when it surges up, disturbs our peace of mind by raising the question as to what shall become of us after death. What is reality? During ordinary moments our minds remain busy with a thousand and one material preoccupations. But in the moments of silence and in the hours of sadness when the mind is inwardly drawn, we begin to think of certain vital questions that have lain dormant during our busy lives.

The blows of misfortune often bring forth a reaction that awakens the soul. Misfortune is, in very many instances, a great teacher of humankind. All the troubles and tribulations that come to us are helpful in the long run. They awaken our inner self and open our mind's eye to the realities of the situation. Besides enlarging our vision they enrich our minds. If we never had any misfortunes or sufferings we could never learn the true nature of this earthly life, and we would not attempt to reach for the highest good. Wise people through their discrimination gain the knowledge that the world is a transitory playground. When they develop this spiritual faculty of mind, they try to get out of the world by following the ancient path of yoga, as pursued by Nachiketa.

Those who have not learned what this world is really like plunge into it with gusto. They enjoy the multitude of pleasures life can offer. But when they find out the hollowness and illusory nature of their enjoyments, they come to know that these are not the true ends of life. By all means, enjoy the pleasures, but be prepared for the reactions, too. One who wishes to receive a mountain of pleasures will have to carry a mountain of miseries as well on his shoulders. When we talk to average people about the path of yoga, which leads to the absolute good, they are sure to look upon us with scorn and indifference. They feel that they have acquired the highest in life, and that those who do not follow their path are missing the mark. But the wise who have renounced the worldly pleasures for the sake of absolute happiness are contented and happy. The conviction is entrenched in their minds that they really do not belong to the world. They attain a progressive realization of their own true nature and for them the entire world becomes a field of *sadhana* and not of *vasana;* that is, of spirituality and not of sensuality.

"Those who are dwelling in the darkness of ignorance and are deluded by wealth and possessions are like children playing with toys. Such foolish children are caught in the snares of death and come again and again under my sway," says the King of Death. "They remain bound in the snares of death. They cannot get beyond the limits of the dark realm. They travel back and forth."

The difference between the departed mortals and the mortals of this plane is that the mortals of this plane are clothed with the garment of flesh, bone, and blood, while the departed souls are clothed with a finer substance of thought and feelings. They can penetrate through a wall, but human beings need a door, and that is the only difference between us and the departed souls. They are just as much within the realm of death as we are. Death means merely a change of our physical garment. It is wrong to think that death means total destruction or absolute annihilation. The wise know that when the transformation of our life takes place, our life reverts to its elementary condition. This means a coming and going. It is the realm of birth and rebirth.

Something can never come out of nothing. There is always a cause behind the effect. Even as a seed hides within itself the gross body of a tree, so is the case with our birth. It is a serious error to imagine that the parents are the creators of human lives. They are but the instruments through which life finds its expression. One may say that God has created the beings, but even He cannot create us out of nothing or send us whimsically from one plane to another, from one condition of existence to another.

Those who do not know where they will find themselves after death are groping in the darkness of ignorance, and are born again and again. One who could know where he was before his present birth could also tell where he would be after his death. Those who search for the inner light and do not stop until the goal is reached, to them the King of Death reveals the mystery of life here and hereafter. Nachiketa, in search of inner light, renounced the transitory realm of pleasure and pain and attained the highest bliss.

When an aspirant goes into samadhi, he transcends the frontiers of death. He realizes a new realm that is beyond death and birth. For those who attain this highest transcendental state, no mystery remains to be disentangled. They see things with new eyes and understand in a new light. For them no question remains unsolved, because they have achieved the light of wisdom. The yoga of the *Kathopanishad* is very difficult to grasp, but those who have faith like Nachiketa will certainly reach their goal. The path of the *Kathopanishad* is not the path of blind followers but of pure *shradhalus* (aspirants).

CHAPTER 5

# *The Metaphysics of Death*

The mystery of death could not be revealed to those who are deluded by wealth and worldly ambitions. Such persons do not seek to realize the true nature of death, and the Ruler of Death declared that they come under his sway again and again. They will be born again, only to die; and will be born to die again and again. The process is repeated until the final liberation is obtained.

The idea of heaven was conceived by the ancient seers of India, but they did not consider heaven as an eternal state, as other religions do. Outside Hinduism and Buddhism, the conception of heaven implies an eternal existence and the continuance of the same condition without end. But according to the belief of the Hindu seers, the heaven or existence after death is not static but is determined variously according to one's own thoughts and deeds. The life in heaven lasts only for a definite period of time. Those who go to heaven to enjoy the celestial pleasures will stay there so long as their good deeds and thoughts entitle them to. There is always a limit to the good deeds and thoughts and there is, therefore, a limit to the results accruing from them.

Eternal heaven, according to Hindu philosophy, is a practical impossibility. The word *eternal* denotes that which is beginningless and endless. According to the rational theory of Vedanta, heaven cannot by its nature be eternal, for all things that are subject to the laws of time, space, and causation are impermanent and perishable. All worldly pleasures are limited by time; they do not continue forever. Celestial pleasures are akin to the pleasures of the world. Even though they may be prolonged for a long time, they must evently come to an end. Those desires that cannot be fulfilled anywhere except in this world will bring us back to this place of existence. This approach is very rational and should appeal to all seekers.

The question asked by Nachiketa about the mystery of death is concerned with the immortal part of our being. All earthly things are perishable. However, if one attains true knowledge by discovering one's own native faculties, one will be able to discriminate between the perishable and the eternal, thus finding the way to eternal bliss, which is the goal of life. The word *immortal* means "that which is not subject to change of any kind." Anything that changes within time and space is mortal. He who desires to know that which is everlasting and unchanging must seek it in a realm beyond the categories of time, space, and causation.

All of us are subject to change, death, and decay because we are born in time and are extended in space and subject to the law of causation. This law applies to the entire phenomenal universe. It exists within time, space, and causation. That is why in the phenomenal universe there is constant change. The seers have found that which is not subject to time and space and transcends the law of causation, which is the *summum bonum* of life and the substratum of this universe. The immortal, the bliss divine, is beyond the reach of death. He who understands this fundamental truth, that the Atman is immortal and all else is perishable, can solve the mystery of death. Death does not mean complete annihilation, it merely means a physical change. Beyond all changes is that immortal part within us.

The common person displays little interest toward the state of immortality. As long as one remains absorbed in worldly pursuits, one cannot attain the wisdom of the immortal Self. The immortal Self is our true and real self. But how many of us pay any attention to it and think of it? Strange to say, "Very few people hear of it and rarer are those who know Him. "In the quest for the realization of immortality, a worthy teacher is as necessary as a worthy pupil. It is indeed wonderful when such a teacher and such a seeker are brought together, but such combinations are few and far between. The spiritual teacher of immortality must be someone quite different from the ordinary preachers and teachers. Those who have not realized themselves cannot reveal truth to others.

The ordinary student of unpurified mind cannot grasp the knowledge of the Atman, even when it is explained by the realized teacher. Before one can realize the highest nature of immortality, one must go through different grades of evolution-physical, mental, and spiritual. There are many who speak about the subject, but when they are asked terse questions about the nature of the real and the unreal, they are simply confused. Knowledge of the scriptures alone will not reveal immortality. One should realize immortality within, and the realization must be the result of continual deep meditation and samadhi.

The practice of yoga is essential in order to achieve this experience and to feel it personally. The unique experience that is attained in samadhi liberates the aspirant from the fear of death. One who has realized his own Atman, and freed himself from the narrow sense of body-consciousness, alone realizes the immortal Self. For him death and life are alike. He dwells in the kingdom of God all the time. This experience can be acquired only through the direct teaching of a realized teacher and not from mere study of scriptures.

The realized guru has the power to open the spiritual eye of the aspirant and to purify his heart and soul. If the seeker's heart, mind, and intellect are not purified, the teacher's effort will not produce the desired effect. Through incessant striving and spiritual longing, the seeker automatically goes through the different stages. An earnest seeker after truth is radically different from the common person. The common person runs after and craves external pleasures such as money, name, and fame, and he is a slave of his own ambitions. But the mind of a true seeker is unconcerned with such material pursuits. He easily grasps truth because of his sincerity, purity, and power of discrimination.

By mere arguments and discussions alone, one cannot understand what exists after death. There cannot be any scientific proof of that absolute truth because it cannot be observed, verified, and demonstrated by sense perception. The immortal Self in us is beyond the reach of sense perception. That which is immortal is subtler than the subtlest. Scientific experiments and logical discussions will not reveal the highest truth, for they have limitations. The scientists cannot, with their scientific approach, reach any concrete conclusions on the immortality of the soul and the life hereafter. Right from the dawn of history, discussion about life after death has been going on, but the truth could not be had from such discussion since it is a truth based on suprasensory awareness. Those who are on the intellectual plane, but are not spiritually awakened, cannot reach any definite conclusion about the immortality of the soul. And nothing can convince them, either. But when the seeker after Truth fortunately meets a realized soul and starts receiving instructions from him, the results are startling. The seeker's doubts are finally removed and he attains wisdom.

**CHAPTER 6**

# *What is Atman?*

The Atman is very subtle, subtler than the subtlest. It is smaller than the smallest. It is finer than the atom. The very existence of the atom depends upon the spiritual principle called the Atman, which is the very foundation of our being. The intense desire that makes an aspirant qualified to receive instruction for realizing the Atman is very difficult to develop. The desire must surge up spontaneously from the depth of our innermost heart. Some persons cherish this precious desire from childhood.

The King of Death told Nachiketa, "You have acquired the intense desire for Self-realization. I have tried to persuade you to give up the third boon and ask for any other boon, such as the joys of heaven and the pleasures of the earth, but you have renounced them all. You have not cared for any of those objects that were offered to you." And then the King of Death imparted the true knowledge to Nachiketa. After the instruction, he discoursed as follows: The thoughts and desires of worldly people lead to transitory results. All these desires and their results are perishable. Those who run after worldly desires come within the realm of death again and again because their ignorance is not dispelled. Those who are convinced of the transitory conditions on this plane do not indulge in worldly pleasures. They know full well that the deeds they perform, whether good or bad, produce but transitory results. Even virtuous and righteous acts cannot produce results that will last forever, for all such results are hemmed in by time and space. Virtuous acts may lead to higher realms such as the abode of ancestors, devas (divine beings), or angels, but all these realms are subject to change. The absolutely unchangeable cannot be obtained by anything that is perishable and transitory. How can one expect to realize the eternal reality by the non-eternal acts of body and mind? One who wants to rise up to the realm of the eternal must rise above all worlds that are non-eternal and non-permanent.

The Atman is not recognizable by the senses. It is hidden within our soul; it dwells in the innermost cavity of our heart; it is deeply buried in the tomb of our body; it is very subtle, very deep and eternal. It existed at the beginning of creation, and exists today, and will exist in the future. If you wish to know this Atman, you must practice the higher steps of yoga. By practicing concentration and meditation you may enter into the super-conscious state (samadhi) and you will come face to face with that which is eternal and immortal. Then you shall be able to realize the Atman, and after this realization you shall rise above pain and pleasure, sorrow and misery. One who realizes that Atman which is seated in the inner chamber of the heart goes beyond all duality and relativity. When the seeker of truth is able to discriminate the immortal from the mortal, he realizes the glory of the Atman. There death has no access, and there is lasting joy and bliss. That realm is the realm of the Absolute, the realm of the Infinite.

The Absolute Being is not far away from us. We have not to go outside of ourselves in search of that absolute Self. We must feel it in our inward depths. We must cut deeper through gross layers, go through progressively subtler spiritual states, and finally enter into the innermost chamber of our own psychic heart, and there we will find the kingdom of Atman.

This is possible only when the student first strengthens the faculty of discrimination. Determination and dedication are two important requisites. The aspirant who has established himself in *dridha sankalpa* (firm determination) and continues his practice fearlessly, one day goes beyond the mire of delusion, beyond all sorrows, misery, and pains.

The aspirant constantly fights several battles to break through the fortress of ignorance. The innermost wall is the wall of ego. The ego, or "I"-consciousness, is very subtle. It is the reflection of the Atman and is subtler than the senses, mind, and intelligence. Most people cannot think of anything beyond it. The whole philosophy of Vedanta, however, is based upon that reality which is beyond the ego and which is divine and immortal. The ego is subject to change, but the divine Self, the Atman, is beyond change and evolution. The changes of the physical body, sense powers, and mind do not affect what lies beyond the ego.

What is that unchangeable principle which is called the Atman? He is impersonally personal. He has no particular form, yet He can assume any form to satisfy the desires and prayers of the devotee. The Brahman is the soul of the universe. Just as our soul is impersonally personal, the Atman has no particular form in us. Similarly, God, being the soul of the universe, has no particular form, and yet He assumes diverse forms. His gross form is the phenomenal universe. He sees through all eyes; He hears through all ears; He feels through all hearts; He thinks through all minds. He pervades the entire cosmos. The Brahman is the soul of the universe; He is the soul of our souls. He who understands this conception of the Atman knows how the Brahman dwells within us. Behind the ego is the Atman, the rider in the chariot of the body. He is like a witness and does not suffer from any change, gross or subtle, physical or mental. He is deathless, but all other things are subject to death. The idea of death so frightening to the ignorant is that death is a state in which everything is annihilated. They know not that the Atman is immortal, and their fear of death is because of their ignorance.

The grand conception of the yoga of the *Kathopanishad* goes deeper than any other philosophy. In no other system is the mystery of death and life hereafter discussed so thoroughly. Those who have no faith in the existence of life after death cannot have a proper understanding of Vedanta, the philosophy of the Upanishads. Skepticism grows out of ignorance; knowledge dispels doubt, as light dispels darkness. The light of knowledge removes the veil of ignorance. So long as we grope in the darkness of ignorance we cannot know anything of the real Self. The Atman is the real immortal Self, the *Purusha*. The ego is the image or the reflection of the Atman. In order to grasp this point, the aspirant should seek the aid of metaphysics, brushing aside erroneous theological theories, dogmas, and doctrines.

Right from the start the student of Vedanta must adopt a spiritual approach to the subject. He is not solely dependent upon mental faculties, for anything within the purview of the mind and the intellect is subject to change and cannot be the highest. A conception of God that functions within the scope of the intellect cannot be the highest object of worship. If God is knowable by the mind and intellect, He is no longer the supreme God. Such a God is a creation of the human mind, a personal God. According to Vedanta, God is unlimited. He is infinite and the source of all intelligence. The Atman is the deepest essence in our Self, and the mind and the intellect have no access to it. We can reach Him only when we have gone beyond intellectual concepts and precepts, ideas and thoughts. We can see Him not by intellectual knowledge but by the divine light.

The Atman is all-pervading. It dwells in all living creatures. It animates everything, from minute particles to the immense solar system. Man is the highest peak of the evolutionary process: in him the manifestation of divinity is more vivid and active than in plants and animals. The human alone is equipped to grasp the truth. To gain the knowledge that God resides in all and that the ego is the reflection of God, non-human creatures have to evolve to the human plane. The human form is the highest product on this plane of existence. It is even higher than the planes of gods and angels, who wish to be born as human beings because they cannot attain Atman without assuming a human body. Human beings can, by their thoughts and deeds, become devas, or divine beings. They alone are capable of experiencing the highest truth or the absolute, which is beyond thoughts. (The plane of the devas is only a realm of thoughts. Devas have thought-bodies, but not physical forms.) Therefore, we human beings should make the best use of the unique opportunities that we have at our disposal.

**CHAPTER 7**

# *The Bliss Immortal*

We have seen how the young seeker Nachiketa was not the least inclined to deviate from his third boon, and how the King of Death was extremely pleased with his zeal and sincerity and taught him the true knowledge. Nachiketa asked the King of Death, "0 Lord, if you are so pleased with me, kindly let me know what is beyond virtue and vice. What is that which is beyond time—past, present, and future?"

The King of Death replied, "All of us have some notions of virtue and vice, but very few know the central something that is beyond the limits of virtue and vice. The sages of all ages and places have tried to discover that something which is beyond all opposites of heat and cold, pleasure and pain, virtue and vice, and so on. The Absolute Reality is beyond our thoughts, desires, and actions."

The Absolute is beyond all phenomena and existence.

Anything we perceive with our senses is an expression of relative existence, that is, existence which is relative to some other existence. We may call it conditional existence. If we examine any event in our life, we will find it related to something else that is not absolutely independent, that in its turn is dependent upon other things outside of itself.

For instance, the sense of pleasure is related to the sense of pain. If one has not suffered from pain, how can one enjoy the bliss of pleasure? Suffering is the pre-condition of pleasant feeling.

Enjoyment is mere comparison. So is the case with knowledge. It all depends on comparison. Had there been no darkness, there would have been no light. According to Vedanta, this dual existence is called *vyavaharika satta,* that is, "one depending upon the other." Within the realm of duality we cannot find the Absolute that is everlasting and unchangeable. Relative existence is subject to change and it extends as far as there is time and space; the Absolute, however, is beyond the flux of relativity.

What are time and space? Time is the interval that exists between two thoughts. A thought arises in our mind and is followed by others, and that succession between the two thoughts is called time. Space means co-existence. Suppose we are aware of something "A" and at the same time think of some other thing "B," and hold these two thoughts together in our mind. That which separates them is called space. Consequently, time and space both depend upon the existence of mental conditions. Analyzing this way, we find that in this phenomenal world everything is within time and space. One who can go beyond them rises above the mental state. So long as there is time, there is space, but after crossing the realms of time and space, we reach the absolute unconditional Reality, without beginning or end. All the phenomenal bodies—like the sun, moon, and earth, and anything we perceive through our senses—have a beginning and consequently must have an end.

Einstein, by his theory of relativity, has proved that since everything in this material universe, from the humblest speck of dust to the mightiest star, is moving in space at tremendous speed, space and time are only relative. There can be no absolute measure of expanding space. He has shown that not only the shape and size of the universe are relative, but our concept of time is also relative, depending as it does upon the velocity of the observer in space. What we call "time" is only a makeshift measurement; the real time is one and indivisible. The concept of endless duration is like our concept of sequential time: hours and minutes are units adopted for the sake of convenience only. In absolute time, there is no past, no future—all is in the present. There can be no dividing line in time as to where the past ends and the future begins. Patanjali defines time as a succession of moments; every moment is in a flux. But for the mind that has realized omnipresence, there is no such succession. Everything has become present for it; to it the present alone exists, the past and future are lost. Time and space are inseparably connected with matter, the sum total of which is the phenomenal world of the four-dimensional space-time continuum. The Absolute is the only reality beyond time and space.

Nachiketa asked about the reality that is beyond time and space, that has neither past nor present nor future. The King of Death replied that there is an absolute Reality which is the background of the phenomenal universe and is described by the scriptures as the highest goal of life. This Reality is unchangeable, beginningless, endless, and all-pervading. The different religions give it different names and forms, but they all point to the one absolute Reality of the universe that is omnipotent and omniscient. These attributes are referred to that one Infinite Being that is the Reality of the universe.

The Vedas and all the scriptures of the world seek the same end. They all describe man's striving after this Reality. They speak of his spiritual aspiration and the methods by which the highest goal can be realized. But mere reading of the scriptures will not help. The aspirant will have to practice the teachings in his life. Reading the scriptures and repeating the mantras mechanically will not do any good until one understands their real spirit and yearns for realization with his whole heart and mind. It is the urge that drives the aspirant to live the life of righteousness, abstemiousness, and truthfulness. All the penances, austerities, and hardships he undertakes are intended to help him realize the fundamental Truth that is the basis of our phenomenal existence.

Different religions have given different names to this absolute Reality. "Eternal Word" is one of its most significant names, and this particular name is used in the Upanishads repeatedly. This Word is the foundation of all our scriptures. All other words have been derived from it, and this Eternal Word is described in the Upanishads as *AUM* (or *Om*). This unique word

Aum, the combination of three letters, is the eternal name of the absolute Reality. The aspirant repeating Aum and contemplating on its meaning understands the absolute Truth. All the phenomenal appearances are based on the foundation of this eternal name, Aum. All desires spring from that infinite source, the absolute Reality, and the fulfillment of all desires depends upon the knowledge of the absolute Reality. One may seek satisfaction of one's desires by the pursuit of worldly pleasures but the satisfaction that is derived will be transient and fleeting. The cravings of the flesh rise up again and again and they bind the human mind and make us unhappy. But when one has acquired the knowledge of the eternal Truth, one's desires are fulfilled in proportion to one's progress toward the goal. The worship of Truth reveals the highest kind of truth and bliss. Even an average man can see that the pleasures he enjoys are not the same as real peace and happiness. Pleasure is not the same as happiness. So long as the mind is troubled by the cares and anxieties of the world, one cannot enjoy the highest joy—the joy divine. Where there is absolute peace, there is expression of true happiness and divine wisdom. It is a difficult state to acquire, but once tasted, it cannot be forgotten. All the yearnings of the aspirant receive their final fulfillment and the resulting satisfaction is everlasting in character.

The sole sustenance of the universe is the absolute Reality.

When one realizes this absolute ground of the universe, one is magnified in the body of the eternal Truth and becomes glorified. A spark of that Reality falling within the realm of time, space, and the laws of phenomenal nature appears as the ego, the thinker, the doer. The true nature of the ego is at one with the absolute Reality, and when, therefore, we understand our true nature, we realize the absolute Truth of the universe.

CHAPTER 8

# *How to Realize the Real Self*

How can we realize our own real Self? First, we must know who we are and what we are in reality, why we have come to this world, where we are going, and what we are going to accomplish by our thoughts and deeds. A person who repeatedly asks himself these questions and tries to solve them satisfactorily will know the value of life, with all its currents and cross-currents.

A great soul cannot remain content without asking and solving such vital questions about the Self and the Reality. But the common man does not have time for these issues. He pursues the phantom of vain hopes and craves for the things that are grossly material, only to be disappointed in the long run. He deludes himself into believing that he is seeking the true substance, while all the time he is only chasing the shadows. All human beings are propelled by a craving for happiness, but they do not know where to find it. Yes, it is only the wise who are able to attain absolute happiness. They have realized that the eternal Self is the symbol of happiness. It is such wise persons, those who have understood the Truth, who live in the eternal bliss, enjoying it every moment of their lives—it is they alone who can lead others safely along the right path.

After divesting themselves of their physical garments, the realized souls go to the abode of infinite wisdom, love, and bliss, enjoying a state of perpetual happiness. The true nature of the Atman is revealed to those who sincerely aspire and work for it.

As long as one labors under false conceptions about the Atman, one cannot gain permanent happiness. Generally speaking, all of us have some vague notions about ourselves that have no relevance to our true Selves. We have vague ideas of the body through which the soul expresses itself. Now, that which provides life and animates it is our real Self. The body itself is a compound of dead matter. The Atman (true Self) is within the body and is also outside of it and separate from it. The body deteriorates and decomposes, but the soul is beyond any such decay. The body may undergo mutations through the process of death and birth, but the Atman remains unaffected. The physical self may suffer, but the real Self is above all turmoils and changes. Those who are deluded with false conceptions about the nature of the Atman suffer in life because they identify themselves with the transitory physical form and body-consciousness.

But the wise seers pursue their thoughts in a different direction. In their quest for Truth they come to realize that the real Self is unborn, imperishable, and immortal by nature, while all the things of the world are transitory and perishable. The Atman, which is the eternal source of all intelligence and wisdom, exists forever, untouched by external mutations. In this phantasmagoria of shifting forms, there is only one that remains unchanged, and that is the real Self. If we look at our body, we will find that it has all along been going through a series of changes and that is how we have become old. Finally, this old body will perish. This is the way the body dissolves and immerses into the ever-recurring process. We are just like a whirlpool. The external matter comes in and the internal matter goes out. It is a constant in-rush and out-rush of material particles. While we take special care of our physical self, we forget that it is nothing but a whirlpool. One who does not forget, however, remains detached from it. Out of ignorance we may concentrate our sole attention upon our physical self, but when we acquire the knowledge of discrimination we will know that the Atman is the only Reality, immortal and eternal. When the eye of wisdom is gradually opened to Truth, we realize that the Atman exists forever and is our permanent abode.

The universe is eternal and therefore its laws are eternal. The highest law, the only Truth, which forms the background of all phenomena, is eternal. Our real Self is also eternal; it is not subject to birth and death. Even after the destruction of the body we shall continue to exist. Nothing can destroy the real Self, for it is beyond the sway of those powers that cause birth, growth, and decay. For instance, take a piece of wood and burn it, and even after destroying the form, the particles of matter that made the piece of wood remain and will remain forever. They are never destroyed. Only the name of the wood and its form are changed, but its reality remains unchanged. So is the case with the body. The reality remains unchanged even after death and the destruction of the body. Therefore, the King of Death told Nachiketa that when the body is dead and destroyed the soul continues to exist. There are spiritual realms where we remain without the help of this physical body or the phenomena around us. They are not cognizable to the sense organs and they can be perceived only through spiritual intuition.

If the slayer thinks that he slays, or the slain thinks that he is slain, he is ignorant of the real nature of the soul. The real Self can neither slay nor be slain. The Atman is indestructible. Fire cannot burn it, water cannot moisten it, air cannot dry it, weapons cannot pierce it. The body may be burnt after death, but the soul continues to exist forever. This is one of the fundamental tenets in the text of the *Kathopanishad*. After death the unrealized souls remain in the realm of the departed ones for an uncertain period. They are not liberated because they could not realize the true nature of their real Self on this plane, and also because they have gone through the ordinary process of death. This process of death does not purify, but merely changes the condition. This change may be painful and lead to a sorrowful state. But death will never be painful if one detaches oneself from the bodily senses and acquires the knowledge of the Atman, which remains impervious to bodily changes.

At the time of death the soul throws away its outer garment, which is the body, as we throw away our soiled clothes and put on new ones. The soul, after fulfilling its desires through the manifestations of the body, throws it away and assumes a fresh form. According to our desires and tendencies, we are born on a higher or lower plane. We must not forget that we are the creators of our future destiny by our thoughts and deeds. It is foolish to think that God punishes the wicked and rewards the virtuous. It is our thoughts and deeds that either punish or reward us. This is a truth centered in the Vedanta philosophy of life.

The real Self, although it may appear in different bodies and under different names, is itself formless and nameless. It is smaller than the smallest and larger than the largest. It is within us and it covers the whole universe. It is the inner dweller of the kingdom of the heart. One can realize it through the grace of the Atman when the mind is fully controlled and made free from worldly temptations. When the heart and mind are fully purified after realizing the true nature of the Atman within, we are free from all sorrows. Misery, pain, and suffering vanish away forever. Anyone who can realize his own Self will be free that very moment from all pains and sufferings. A human being is a child of eternal bliss, and the child inherits all the qualities that the father possesses. The child only needs growth, development, and unfoldment. Wake up from the slumber of ignorance and recognize your true blissful nature. Feel the eternity and be free from sorrow and the fear of death. Know and realize that you are a child of eternal bliss. Feel it and be always conscious of it. One should first realize one's own real Self and the rest will take care of itself. The fear of death is like a timekeeper who reminds you to complete your joy here on this plane. Death is never painful. It is a change in which one's true nature is not changed; death changes the outer garment of the soul.

One may gain worldly pleasures, but they will not bring happiness to one. Material things cannot reveal the nature of the true Self, and it is for this reason that the wise renounce the world and become free from all worldly ties. When they fully realize that these worldly things will not bring them happiness and will not make them free from the fear of death, renunciation becomes a matter of joy for them. It is the ignorant and the self-deluded who care for the momentary worldly pleasures. Those who are attracted by the charms and temptations of the objects of the senses simply fool themselves. They are responsible for their follies and therefore they suffer. All sufferings and pains spring from ignorance, while happiness springs from knowledge. It is knowledge that brings the highest bliss.

One would rather die a thousand times than live ignobly in a state of ignorance. But if one gains that knowledge which is capable of lifting one above this worldly plane, then one should consider oneself fortunate. One who has reached this final aim of life has fulfilled the aim of this earthly existence. One may pray and worship God, but all the prayers and worship will be of no avail unless one learns by experience that the plane on which one lives is not one's own but belongs to God, and one is simply an instrument in the hands of the mighty Self. Very few know the technique and the art of living in this world. He who lives in this world knowing that he has come here to realize the Self and that the world and its phenomena are the means to achieve his end is free from all sorrows and free from the fear of death. He who wants liberation should strive earnestly in this very life and liberate himself. He should not wait until he is laid into the grave when his body perishes and his bones are turned to dust.

Our individualized and differentiated beings are continuously sustained by the very substance that is the support of the phenomenal world. That Reality is eternal, beginningless, and everlasting. If we are able to understand that the eternal, the endless, and unchangeable is the source of our intelligence, the basic unity in diversity is perceived. The individual ego is only a manifestation of the eternal substance through the framework of phenomenal existence.

There are three conditions of phenomenal existence: namely, time, space, and causation. In Sanskrit they are called the three different aspects of *maya*. One who can rise above these three conditions shall discover the eternal imperishable Atman. But it is extremely difficult to do so, because of our very existence. This world involves the limitations of space, time, and the law of causality. Anything that exists within time cannot remain stationary, and therefore is subject to the evolutionary process of growth, decay, and death.

Life and death are only different names for the same fact—the two sides of one coin. Ultimately saneness and distraction are one and the same. Death and birth are auxiliary to the one Reality. As long as good and evil exist in a person's mind he cannot transcend the realm of death, but when he gets rid of both good and evil, he can have bliss. A human being is immortal in his true nature. He is infinite, without beginning and without end: the ever-moving ripple in an infinite ocean of the joy of divine bliss.

An adamantine wall shuts a human being in egotism until he gives up the world manufactured by evil. Never until then can he enter the kingdom of heaven; none ever did nor ever will. The person who has purified himself thoroughly accomplishes in a day that which is not possible for thousands of men in a hundred or even a thousand years. Out of purity comes bliss. Man is certainly not other than his own focus; but he can see only his reflection and never the real thing. Purity, sincerity, faithfulness, truthfulness, and constant meditation lead aspirants to the highest reality, where death has no access.

Our physical bodies are subject to birth, growth, decay, and death, like all other gross material things. Birth is followed by death. This is the inexorable law of the phenomenal world. We cannot retain the physical self forever; some day it must pass away. We are evolving constantly from one state of change into another. Physically, we are not the same creature twice. Our physique and mind constantly change. In this realm of change we cannot find anything that is immortal, because anything that is subject to birth and growth cannot be immortal. This is the immutable law of nature. Immortality, therefore, is to he found only beyond the realm of time, space, and causation.

In the course of their investigations, materialistic thinkers cannot find anything that is unchangeable and imperishable. Therefore, they cherish the dictum that "eat, drink and be merry" is the only aim of life and that there is nothing else apart from it. They also assert that there is no such thing as an unchangeable existence. They proclaim in the bold negative that life in this world is the happiest that can be imagined. They believe that, inasmuch as all the things of the world are constantly changing, there can be nothing beyond this, nothing that is eternal and immortal. The materialistic way of life and thinking is confined wholly to the conditions of time, space, and causation. One who practices this superficial theory of the agnostic and the atheist cannot expect to be free from grief and sorrow here in this world and hereafter.

The King of Death says that the ego is something that is immutable. The ego is a reflection of the Atman, which is immortal and unchangeable and very difficult to grasp because it lies hidden and secret deep in the breasts of human beings. To know the Atman we have to have a sharp intellect, pure heart, and a keen sense of discrimination. The aim of all seekers after Truth is to reach the highest goal. The real seeker is not satisfied with the relativity of the changeable world.

## CHAPTER 9

# *The Source of Consciousness*

The quest for Truth is the beginning of religion. All religions seek to lead their followers to Truth. Though they may express it under various names and forms, their chief objective is to reach that unchangeable Brahman which is man's supreme destiny and final goal.

Vedanta is a philosophy, but it is also a living religion, a religion of humanity. It deals with the ultimate questions of human life and answers them satisfactorily, enabling the human mind to attain happiness, wisdom, and bliss *(sat-chit-ananda)*.

Anyone who searches within himself in all sincerity and purity of heart can discover this truth. The highest abstraction, in which all things are harmonized, is one Absolute—all pervading. In religion we have first symbols and forms, next mythology, and last philosophy. The first two serve a temporary purpose. Philosophy is the underlying basis of all, and the other means are only stepping-stones in the struggle to reach the ultimate goal. Books cannot teach God, but they can help the aspirant in destroying the ignorance in a negative way. A state comes when the aspirant has to unlearn all the learning and go beyond scriptural knowledge.

If you sit in solitude and study closely your own self, you will gradually begin to be aware of that consciousness which is your own being. This consciousness is passed on from childhood to youth, from youth to maturity, and from maturity to old age. You remain essentially the same person and your identity remains the same. This sameness, however, is not rooted in matter, because matter is constantly changing. Nor is it contained in energy, because energy is also changing. The divine consciousness, however, does not change at all. Of course, the state of consciousness undergoes various gradations.

The source of consciousness is always the same, unchangeable and immortal. It is the source of our intelligence. It is shedding its light, making you feel that you exist at every step. At every moment of your life you are fully aware of your existence. It is the cause of the knowledge of your own being or existence. The Atman is the witness of all the changes of the world. For instance, if you sit quietly and watch your mind, you will find that all of a sudden a thought bubbles up. It rises and goes away, but another comes up and takes its place and plays a different part and then also goes away. Each idea or sensation or perception comes like a picture and you watch it. So is the case with all passions, hatred, and anger. They all vanish one after another. But still you are the same witness to all these mental metamorphoses. That reality, the witness, cannot be established by any scientific method, for scientific observations and experiments depend entirely upon sense perception. On the other hand, the witness who constantly watches all the changes, outer and inner, is beyond the realm of sense perception, the mind, and the ego. The power through which we perceive the sense objects is quite different from that of the senses and their objects.

Scientific precepts and concepts cannot reveal that witnessing power which is seated in the innermost chamber of our heart. For instance, the chain is illumined by the light, but if you wish to study the light, the chain will not help you. In the same way, sense perception will not help you in studying your own Atman. The senses cannot reveal the Truth, for Truth is revealed by itself. If a part of your limb is paralyzed and if that part is then cut off, you will not feel its absence. Thus, it is the self-conscious ego that reveals all sense perceptions.

Science deals only with the realm of sense perceptions. It cannot explain the mystery of the Self. Philosophy begins where science ends. Philosophy is in fact a more systematized and organized study than science. Science is particularized knowledge of a certain part, while philosophy is the integrated knowledge of the whole. It accepts all the conclusions of the different branches of science, unifies them organically, and yields a truth that is beyond the scope of science. Therefore, if we wish to know the unchangeable entity within us, we cannot get much help from a study of the different branches of science. One must learn to study oneself. He who seeks to find out who he is and what he is, to him the study of philosophy will reveal the knowledge of the Atman. He who understands his immortal nature, the true significance of immortality, reaches the kingdom of immortality. After a careful study of the philosophy of life, the seeker will find that the Atman is without beginning and end. The body has its beginning and end, but not the Atman. The Atman is birthless and deathless.

As we cannot think of our beginning or of the time when we did not exist, so we cannot think of the time when we shall cease to exist. Consciousness is the inherent essence of our being, and it is deathless. It was never born. The Reality that is birthless and deathless is beyond the process of beginning and dissolution. Anything and everything in this world that is subject to birth must go through the process of constant change, must decay and die. A plant is born of a seed. It grows, decays, and dies. So also birth is followed by growth, decay, and death. Our Atman is never born, it does not grow, nor is it ever subject to decay and destruction. Perfection belongs to our vital stuff. If we do not feel it, it is because of our lack of insight into the truth of our immortal nature. He who knows and realizes that he is divine, a part of the Absolute which is perfect, knows that he is the child of Immortal Bliss. Of course, it takes a long time, and ceaseless practice and patience, to understand the illimitable potentialities, in one's personal life, of our Atman. Most of us mechanically repeat the great truth that we are the children of God without knowing its deep meaning—but once we grasp its true import we tend to become perfect.

The King of Death explained to Nachiketa that the Atman,

within the city of human life, is birthless, deathless, and indivisible. It is all Intelligence and, therefore, the basis of all intelligence and knowledge. One may imagine that one derives knowledge externally by experiments and observations, but no knowledge can emanate from outside of ourselves. Knowledge comes from within. The external phenomena can only give suggestions, and in response or reaction we draw the knowledge from within. Some minds do not, however, react properly because of the darkness of ignorance that encircles them. In Sanskrit this is called *tamasa,* which means dullness or stupidity. It is something like a layer of dust on the mirror of intelligence. Removing it helps the aspirant in achieving his goal. Without removing this dust, the knowledge of the Atman cannot be acquired.

In other words, the knowledge is already there in every one of us, but it is for us to make the necessary effort to recognize it. When this recognition is effected, knowledge springs forth from the source of all knowledge within, the Supreme Intelligence which is the witness of all our thoughts and deeds. It has not accrued out of anything, because it is itself the Divine Intelligence. The moment we know our own Being, all knowledge is revealed to us and the mystery of death and birth is solved. The reality of a human being is not in what he reveals to others, but it is in what he cannot reveal to others. Therefore, one who wishes to understand another should not listen to what he says but rather study what he does not say. Half of what we say is meaningless; half of what we do is also meaningless. The other half within us, which remains expressionless, is the vital part to be studied. The real in us is silent. The moment we realize that the Atman resides in us, we will be able to render true service to humanity. We all are children of Immortal Bliss.

Vedanta postulates the immanence of the unchangeable Reality amidst the changing universe. It is absurd to think that we die and suffer, when we really are free from death and sufferings. No one can make us immortal if we are not immortal already.

That source of knowledge and intelligence, by which we know, exist, and act, is our real Self. If we know our Self, we know the whole universe, we know God, we know that the essence of God is the same as the Atman. The realization of God's existence is inseparable from the knowledge of our Self. If He does not exist, how can we exist? The very knowledge of our existence depends on our being in a state of consciousness. The real Self cannot die. It continues to exist even when the physical self is destroyed. The physical self is the gross medium that remains latent in the Atman. When the body is destroyed, the subtle substance of the body remains the same. Nothing is destructible. The form of the Devil can be destroyed, but what is destroyed is merely form and name. So the name and form of the body is susceptible to destruction, but the real Self within remains unchanged. A person is like a wave in the ocean of bliss. When the wind blows, the wave vanishes as if it had never been; but its rising and falling in the ocean does not destroy its existence. Thus the lives of human beings are blown away by death. The reality of life is Life itself, whose beginning is not the ovum and whose end is not the grave. Life itself is a continuous existence from eternity to eternity. Death is a revealer, a guide, and a torch-bearer. Death is a habit of the body and not of the soul. It rounds out life's tragedies. Our main difficulty is that we live thinking and brooding on our past. Either we brood on the past or we imagine our future. Thus we lose our present, which is the golden link between past and future. Past and future do not affect the person who lives in the present. Those who live in the present are free from all the bondages of transitory changes of the world. Those who know that all the things of this world are mortal and subject to change, understand the value of the recurring changes of this world.

If while this recurring change and death of the physical self is going on we do not seek to realize our great Atman, we fail to fulfill the purpose of life. We cannot be happy unless we realize our immortal Self, unless we free ourselves from the cycle of death and birth, thus becoming devoid of all our imperfections. "If the killer thinks that he kills and if the killed thinks that he is killed, both of them do not know that the soul can neither kill nor be killed." The Bhagavad Gita explains it admirably. The conception is unique and is not found elsewhere. The indestructibility of the Self is a fundamental tenet in Vedanta philosophy. Students will find it easier to understand and accept this principle only as they accustom themselves to the lofty ideals of the Upanishads.

CHAPTER 10

# *The Terrestrial Plane Ephemeral*

The unchangeable Atman dwells in each heart. It is eternal Truth. Search your heart and you will find it. After finding it, you will not and cannot lose the Reality. You may lose the physical self and with it all your worldly relations, but you will find that Existence is real, divine, and eternal. He who has realized his Atman does not crawl on this earth, but strides over it majestically, secure in his realization that he is the proud possessor of the bliss immortal. Difficult though the acquisition of the knowledge of the Atman is, it is yet the only true objective. This objective can surely be achieved if you yearn for it and if you set about the quest with single-minded concentration and purity of heart.

On this terrestrial plane of ours everything is superficial and ephemeral. Our senses are so deceptive, our mind is so limited, and our intellect so circumscribed, that we remain stuck with the objects of the world. But the wise, whose vision transcends the petty pains and pleasures of the earth, can see the Truth in all its grandeur beyond the pleasures and pains of the earth. The Atman, though essentially changeless, is constantly manifesting itself through the body. Whoever knows the glory of the Atman already finds himself in the kingdom of bliss and immortality. He enjoys perennial peace and happiness. He has realized his Atman and has become immortal.

The King of Death says, "It (the Atman) is beyond words."

This eternal Truth cannot be acquired by studying the scriptures alone, though all the scriptures claim to reveal the highest Truth. They are at best only an attempt to register the highest Truth. They can give vision, but not the Reality in its entirety. The Vedas and the Upanishads as well as all the sacred scriptures of the world cannot by themselves reveal the Truth. One may read the scriptures for years at a stretch but this study by itself will not help the seeker in realizing Truth. One may get an idea and visualize certain things, but visualization is not realization. Mere words cannot show the reality of the Atman. They are but the outward expressions of our thoughts when we cannot experience the absolute Reality. How can it be expected that words could reach it? Where thoughts end, there is the absolute Reality. Thoughts are always on the plane of relativity. Thoughts are related to our "I "-consciousness or ego. If there is no thinker, there can be no thoughts. Thoughts are nothing but the products of the ego; things of this world are thoughts of the cosmic mind. For instance, the sun, moon, and stars are not of the finite minds, but are the thoughts of the cosmic mind. Thus all the scriptures of the world are not capable of revealing the real nature of the absolute Truth. If the study of the scriptures by itself could have revealed truth, then all those who studied them should already have realized it.

The scientific approach can take us a long way along the road to knowledge, but there is a line beyond which it cannot proceed. Any intellectual flight into the realm of the absolute Truth is merely playing with words. Access to the Atman can be had, not through the intellect, but through a purified heart filled with intense zeal and with a one-pointed mind. In the process of cosmic evolution humankind has been given a guide that is called reason. When reason speaks to a person's inmost self, he knows the real worth of his desires and thoughts; he knows the purpose of life. In the path of realization, reason is a prudent minister, a royal guide, and a wise counselor. Reason is light in darkness, but is helpless without the aid of knowledge—the knowledge of Self (Atman) and non-Self (an-Atman). The knowledge of Atman and an-Atman is the first stage of Self-realization. Unless this faculty of discrimination is strengthened, nothing is possible.

Truth, goodness, justice, and love avail little if the faculty of discrimination is discarded; this would be just like an unarmed soldier proceeding to the battlefield. The learned man who has not developed the faculty of discrimination and tries to lead others is a case of the blind leading the blind. The light of discrimination is a constant guide in an aspirant's life. God has given this marvelous faculty to humankind so that by its light each may not only worship God but also see in ourself our weakness and our strength. Blessed are those on whom God has conferred the gift of discrimination. The great Vedic seers have affirmed that through pure consciousness alone the knowledge of everything becomes possible.

People struggle and strive hard to accumulate wealth, power, and possessions. But they will be of no consequence to a person at the time of his death when oblivion sets in. When he dies, they will all disappear from him like a dream. A wealthy man who is hoarding wealth all his life carries with him even after death his passion for gold. Though he will not find any gross substance like gold after his departure, yet his inordinate desire will burn in him even after death and he will suffer because it cannot be translated into its gross material form. For how can one enjoy the pleasure of dancing when there is no dance? Such a state of existence is obviously not a very pleasant one. It is well to remember that such an unpleasant state is brought into being by our own desires. Our worldly desires become rooted in the deepest recesses of our mind and we carry their burden even after death. Alas! All the material objects, all the gross forms of our desires by which we gratified ourselves, must remain in this world only.

Most of us do not think of the Reality and thus waste the precious time of life. We generally live in the thoughts of the past and the future. We misuse our present by acting foolishly, by recalling the dead past and visualizing an uncertain future. We are not vigilant and wise in our behavior, for we know not that life is nothing but time. Those who do not prepare themselves right now to face the conditions that may arise in the future or the life after death are foolish persons digging their graves with their own hands. Only after Self-realization can one solve the mystery of life here and hereafter. After realization this universe of ours appears like a dream and the body is like a prison-hole.

The path of knowledge is the path of divine love. Love that does not renew itself every day becomes a mere habit and turns into slavery. True love is something higher than worldly love. True love is love divine and love for God. When the devotee starts loving the Highest, divine love begins to manifest itself. Human love is a reflection of the divine love and it manifests through the sense plane. The imperfections of the sense plane distort the divine love and that is how we get so mixed up and become unable to discriminate between divine love and human affection or attachment. We often mistake the one for the other, thus inviting upon ourselves all the miseries and sorrows of the world.

Human love is quite different from the love of God. If human love and love for God or the divine were one and the same, there would have been no pain and misery in the world, because every human being has in him some kind of love for some kind of object. While human love diminishes and becomes static, divine love produces perennial joy. As all worldly objects are changing, our love for them also undergoes changes. When we withdraw our mind from the objects of the world and focus it on God alone, we will realize what that highest form of love is. We can acquire this love if we cultivate a longing for it. Intense longing is the way to God-realization, for no such longing remains unfulfilled.

But divine love cannot be had so long as one has not experienced with one's discrimination that this phenomenal world is made of ever-changing names and forms. One who knows the nature of the phenomenal world has understood the laws that govern phenomenal life, and once this is learned all worldly charms lose their values. However valuable the worldly goods may seem from a material point of view, they become insignificant when the longing for the highest Truth animates us. Worldly objects will always pull us down unless we possess the power of discrimination, renunciation, and detachment. Those who have renounced the world have done so because they found that relatives and friends and possessions were obstacles in the path of spiritual realization. When renunciation comes, when the resolve becomes rock-like, all our external relationships lose their individual idiosyncracies and coalesce in our identification with God. In such a state of mind, everything around us becomes saturated in divinity. To him who sees the reality of things in the light of divinity, the whole material world, with all its relations and attractions, vanishes. This huge caravan of earthly life becomes a dream.

A dream, however, is as real as the waking state, unless we wake up. It is hard to achieve this state of waking so long as we are in the dream of ignorance. But there comes a time in every person's life when he feels that everything he has experienced during his lifetime has faded away like a dream, leaving only a cloud of impressions. Those on whom misfortune has dealt the harshest blows can better understand the clear distinction between the waking and the dreaming states of life. The blows of adversity serve as teachers and friends for those who are wise. While the pleasant things of the world keep us immersed in our delectable dream, it is adversity that awakens us to the rock-bed of reality.

The knowledge that neither teaches us the value of things as they are nor makes us free from the bondage of the world is not real knowledge, for such knowledge will never come near Truth. There are various grades of knowledge. The appearance of the world, language, and action are never greater than ourselves. The Atman is our final abode, our eyes are its windows, and language is its messenger. The knowledge based on sense-perception is not its complete expression. The knowledge that becomes a guide comes from the depth of consciousness that is enriched by discrimination. Such knowledge becomes a faithful companion who never fails. Reality cannot be known without the help of discriminative knowledge, and this knowledge cannot be obtained without purity of mind.

Unless one corrects and purifies one's heart and mind, one cannot know Reality. If there be the slightest longing for anything on the material plane, one cannot grasp the divine. He will be tied to earth. He who is full of desires must gratify them first and be rid of them through experience. We have come to this world to learn through experience. He who has acquired enough experience will not become a slave of his desires by running after fresh pastures. He is wise who turns his mind away from worldly temptations and uncontrolled desires and directs it toward Self-realization. When we dive deep into ourselves and are poised and balanced, we come to know that life is not merely a dream, that it has also its purpose, which must be realized and fulfilled. We have come to this plane to fulfill this purpose and achieve our final aim. He who studies in silence about his purpose and his own Self, and ponders over what he has accomplished and how much he has gained, knows the real value of life. No one can hide anything from his own Self. All of us are our own masters. We have to redeem ourselves by becoming our own redeemers. If we allow petty things to attract our attention and disturb our peace of mind, we make ourselves unsuitable to know the Highest. He who makes his mind firm as a rock and remains unmoved by the storms of life acquires the requisite mental equipoise to accomplish his purpose in life. The weak are not fit to enter the kingdom of heaven because they are driven hither and thither by every gust of wind, by every kind of passion, desire, and ambition. Only those who remain unruffled by the rush and roar of the world become victorious in the end.

**CHAPTER 11**

# *The Absolute and Its Relation to the Universe*

The teachings of religion are very simple, but we have made religion highly complex and hideous by ignorantly following distorted doctrines and dogmas. Truth and love are the twin tenets taught by all religions, and each religion has its own way of emphasizing them, depending upon its particular outlook and the needs of the times. The basic principles are one and the same for all religions, but the human mind has multiplied them and made them look different and even mutually contradictory. Religion is the relationship between a human being and God, and if this aspect is understood, the purpose of religion is served. Most people lead their lives covered with several layers of conceit and superstition. Truth stands away from the follies of the human mind. Should anyone possess the power to rise above superstitions, him Truth will embrace.

The ultimate aim of the student of yoga is to attain the state of samadhi. In samadhi, the jiva (the individual soul) and Brahman are united. Samadhi means God-consciousness. He who is conscious of truth and practices it in thought, word, and deed is in the divine all the time. The greatest obstacle on the path of samadhi is the ego. But when one casts off one's ego, one will realize that the source of all intelligence behind the mind and the ego is the Atman. Such a person attains eternal freedom. But he whose mind is constantly distracted by the things of the world forgets his own Self and clings to his beloved ego. For the student of yoga all the worldly attractions are temporary and do not amount to anything worthwhile. He learns his lessons from the fleeting pleasures of the world and gets out of their clutches in time. He does not waste his lifetime by following the footprints of the atheists whose motto is "Eat, drink, and be merry." He does not follow such hollow ideals and attractions. As long as a person is immersed in the darkness of ignorance, he is full of desires and ambitions; for him everything is attractive. But after gaining diverse experiences in life, he finds his former attractions repulsive. He then begins to think of something higher and nobler than that which he has experienced so far.

The absolute Brahman swallows up all the names and forms of this transitory plane. On this plane death destroys everything, but Brahman, the highest, destroys death too. The destroyer of death is the absolute Brahman, from whom spring all the things of this world. All the phenomena on the sense plane and the mental plane are swallowed up by Brahman. The absolute Brahman eats up, as it were, all these things, and death is but a condiment. The moment one detaches oneself from the external world, all the pulls and powers of the latter are gone. It is only our imagination that gives color and sound to worldly sensations. In our ignorance we cannot see the worldly objects for what they really are. He who withdraws his mind from the organ of hearing hears not any sound and is enveloped in silence. He who takes away his mind from the sense of touch will not feel heat or cold. This world is a creation of our five senses, and when the mind is withdrawn from these five senses, the same world that we feel, see, and touch will vanish.

He who is capable of analyzing his own perceptions is above the realm of deceptions and illusions. He who sees things as they really are lives in harmony with reality. But those who pursue superficial idols and phantoms pay the penalty. For those who live on the surface, such attractions may seem quite powerful indeed. But from the standpoint of the true aspirant they are futile and transitory, because they do not clean the mind or enrich the soul. Our whole life with all its experiences makes up our character. All the experiences that we gather on this plane vanish after death but leave their essential imprint upon our character, which persists even after physical death in the form of the subtle body. Death is capable of laying waste the flowers but is unable to harm the seeds. We accumulate a great variety of such imprints through our previous experiences. They are with us and will remain with us in the future, also.

Everything that we have enjoyed and suffered has left its stamp upon the mind, and this impression furnishes the cause of future desires of a similar nature, thus forging the endless causal chain of desires and their experiences. Anyone who examines carefully his own life should be able to discover the compulsive forces in his character. When a sensation that has already been enjoyed is repeated, one feels a sense of helplessness to stop it. This only serves to show that the character that has been built up by our thoughts and deeds is subtler than our gross body. By our character we create our destiny and our future. Whatever we have sown we reap in the future. This law is inexorable and we are all bound and chained by it. Whatsoever one thinks and experiences comes under the law of action and reaction, of cause and consequence, at every moment of life. The law is: As you sow, so shall you reap. The whole world is built upon this law that we experience every day. He who wants to know the mystery of death and rebirth must first understand this law of karma. Ordinarily students think that the word *karma* means action. That is true, but the rope of karma has three cords—the gross is of action, the finer is of thought, and the finest is of desires. These three cords twisted into one have made the strong rope of karma. Karma means action, thought, and desire. To cut the strong rope of karma is to eliminate thoughts and desires also and not only to control and purify the actions.

By doing selfless and skillful actions the grosser cord of action is removed, and by meditation the finer cord of thought is removed. By knowledge of the Self alone the finest cord of desire is removed. Until then a person remains in the bondage of karma. The law of karma is inevitable for all; but for the realized soul it remains bondage no longer.

This very law of karma, when directed toward spiritual perfection by yoga practices, helps the aspirant to attain concentration of mind and to uncover hidden mental and physical powers, thus leading him to enter into conscious communion with the Lord of the heart, and facilitates the progress toward liberation from physical bondages. Yoga is the master key to reopen secret realms of eternal bliss and peace. The highest steps of yoga doubtlessly transmute the keen aspirant into a divine personality. The ultimate aim of yoga is the spiritual union between the individual soul and the supreme Self. And thereby even the law of karma is transcended. As a huge pile of fuel wood brought into contact with fire is reduced to ashes, similarly all the karmas and errors of the aspirant are reduced to ashes by the fire of knowledge. Knowledge liberates the aspirant. Selfless action leads to this knowledge. There is no bondage for the person who has acquired the knowledge of the Atman.

CHAPTER 12

# *The Nexus Between the Absolute and the Ego*

The King of Death, having described the Absolute and its relation to the universe, goes on to explain the nexus between the Absolute and the ego. The King of Death says, "The one (the Absolute) is like the self-effulgent sun, the other (ego) is like its image or reflection, bearing relations as between light and shade. The one is like a witness, while the other eats the fruits of its own thoughts and deeds." There are two things within us: one, the eternal absolute Self, the imperishable substance; and the other, the little self—the ego, which is the thinker, the enjoyer, and the sufferer. The relation between the two is that of the sun to its reflection. The Absolute is self-resplendent, unaffected, and unchanged. The clouds may cover the sun, but it is never affected or disturbed. It is not affected when human eyes cannot see it on a rainy day. In like manner, the absolute Self remains embedded in the cave of our heart in all its glory. That shrouded Reality, that Absolute Substance, is the Atman. The ego is merely an image or reflection. It works through the body and the senses and is conscious of all activities connected with the physical organism. The ego, which is the thinker or enjoyer, reaps the results of its thoughts and deeds, while the Atman remains like a witness. When one's mind is covered with the cloud of hatred, that witness stands immune to it. The ego thinks, "I want this, I have that, I love this," and so on. These thoughts and feelings appear and disappear in the mind, but the absolute Reality remains unaffected like the sun.

The ego is the reflection or the image of the Atman. As the reflection of the sun cannot be had if there be no sun, so also the ego cannot exist without the Atman. An image or reflection depends for its causation upon the original thing. For instance, the face that you see in a mirror does not exist by itself but is dependent on your face. In like manner, the ego cannot exist independently of the Atman. The King of Death explains this with a beautiful illustration, which was subsequently employed by Plato. In a beautiful simile the Atman or the real Self has been compared with the rider of a chariot. The chariot is the gross body, the intellect is the charioteer, the mind is the reins, the senses are the horses, and the objects of the senses are the roads. While the intellect is driving this chariot, the real Self or the Atman is the witness seated apart and watching the intellect, the mind, and the sense perceptions.

The King of Death teaches that when the highest Spirit is in union with the body, senses, and mind, such a person is a true enjoyer. The ego is that state in which the rider is closely allied with the intellect, the mind, and the sense powers. So long as the mind, the intellect, and the sense powers prevail, he is the enjoyer, the thinker, and the doer. But one who can cross the realms of the mind, the intellect, and the ego, and thus pass into the state of trance, is free forever. The body, the mind, and the intellect are but the instruments the ego uses to gain experience and fulfill certain desires. As long as we remain within the realm of the ego, we cannot help struggling and reaping the results of our thoughts and deeds.

There are some vital questions before the human mind, such as the purpose behind birth and rebirth and the meaning of death and life after death. A right answer to these vital questions leads us to the knowledge of the mystery of death. The ordinary person often gets lost in seeking to grasp this most subtle and abstruse subject. The scriptures seek to explain the true nature of the Atman, but we find ourselves amidst a bewildering diversity of interpretations on this theme. The Christians say that God created humankind in His own image. The reference is not to the human body, which is imperfect. If human bodies were created by God in His own image, then He would also share these physical limitations and imperfections in common with His creation. It is wrong to argue that if human beings are the image of God, He must also look like a human being. This conception is shockingly primitive.

A careful study of Vedanta should serve to bring out the true meaning of the scriptures. According to Vedanta it is the ego that is the individual soul and that is the image of God. God is universal Spirit. He is like a sun, and each individual soul is like a reflection of the sun on the mirror of cosmic intelligence. As a reflection cannot exist without an object, so also the individual soul cannot exist unrelated to the spirit whose reflection it is. If we are the reflections or the images of God, we must also partake of His nature. According to Vedanta, the Atman is within us and around us, though He is not visible to the naked eye. The materialists try to understand God through sense perceptions, and when naturally they fail in their efforts, they deny the very existence of the Atman. The ego is like a bridge that we have to cross to go to the other shore—to the kingdom of the Atman. We cannot reach the realm of divinity in any other way except over the bridge of ego. Therefore he who wants to know God should know himself. We cannot attain immortality unless we cross the bridge of our ego.

We can grasp the nature of our ego by means of analysis and by studying ourselves. Each individual must find out for himself where the Atman is and what it is like. Those who live on the sense plane and who delude themselves by erroneous thinking cannot know the Atman. So long as one slumbers in self-delusion, one cannot see the blissful way to the kingdom of the divine. But when one is awakened and makes genuine efforts in all sincerity and purity of mind and heart, achievement is rendered easy.

Let's revert to the illustration of the body as a chariot. In this chariot the intellect, which is the charioteer, is responsible for all the good and evil thoughts that are received. If the driver is not careful and the horses are not properly trained, they might become unruly and drag the chariot down into the ditch. If the driver does not possess the competence to control the horses, the ego suffers. But if the driver knows the right direction and the right way to handle the horses, there will be no mishaps. A person whose mind is unbridled cannot control his senses, and he succumbs to them. In the absence of severe self-control the senses get the upper hand and drag the charioteer in any direction they like. An uncontrolled mind is like a bird with broken wings that falls into the river of passion and is carried along with the current to the deep ocean of sorrow.

All kinds of follies and crimes are committed by those who are not self-controlled. They could save themselves from much avoidable pain and suffering if only they would exercise their intelligence and desist from the mad pursuit of sensory pleasures. He who exercises self-control will have a firm grip over the reins of the mind. His mind obeys him as diligently as the horses submit to a capable charioteer. If a person is overpowered by the attractions of the world, it is because the driver has not first disciplined himself. He who does not exercise his power of discrimination and is always slothful and impure can never attain perfection and must wallow in the world of imperfections. If one is not mindful of one's own Self and one's own duties, one cannot attain perfection. To achieve perfection, the first requisite is purity of mind and of the senses. Without exercising self-control and discrimination, none can hope to reach the kingdom of heaven. To those who understand the moral, mental, spiritual, and physical laws properly, the way to heaven is always open.

But most people are devoid of discrimination. If a person does not exercise his faculty of discrimination, he cannot differentiate between right and wrong. While right discrimination is very valuable, even for material advancement, it is much more so in the path of contemplation. When a high degree of discrimination is developed, pure and noble thoughts come to occupy our mind and help us in Self-realization. It is well to remember that in order to purify the mind and heart one should cultivate the habit of cherishing holy thoughts. Everything that is elevating and beneficial to humankind and that makes a person selfless, everything that helps a person in developing conscious self-denial, is to be pursued as the ideal of life. Self-denial helps one in expediting one's progress on the path of yoga. The more one gives, the more one receives. He who makes the firm resolution that he shall never do any wrong to anyone, however much he may have been injured, is on the right road to Self-realization.

If all humans were only trained from infancy toward self-denial, we would have established the kingdom of heaven on this plane. A tender bamboo can easily be bent to shape, but it is difficult to do so when its rings have become thickened. Unfortunately, what we find today is that our children, instead of imbibing the rules of right conduct and right aspiration, are taught only how to become clever enough to obtain material success at the expense of others. The student of yoga should exercise discrimination and self-control at every moment of life. Practice self-denial and you will find that you have risen above the level of ordinary humans. Those who eschew personal aggrandizement command the respect of society. The way to prosperity, godliness, and spirituality is the way of right knowledge and self-control.

The common person thinks that perfection implies a kind of heaven where he enjoys all sorts of pleasures without having to take any pains at all. This absurd idea is cherished by most people. Perfection means a state of equilibrium in which all the senses and passions are effectively integrated and controlled, thus allowing the attainment of absolute command over oneself. In this state of perfection the past, present, and future are fully revealed. All the gross and subtle laws that govern the physical and mental planes become easily intelligible to us. All our questions will be solved at this stage. This state of equilibrium is absolutely essential for achieving the highest in life. Self-control, self-denial, and right knowledge—anyone possessing these three virtues will attain self-realization. Whether one believes in God or not, if only one possesses these qualities, one will achieve the highest perfection, which is the goal of life. Blind belief in God is poor consolation and cannot be of much help on the path of liberation. Belief should be accompanied by right knowledge of discrimination. Blind faith not only doesn't help, it is an obstacle to realization. Only that faith is helpful which is kindled by the right knowledge of discrimination, and such a faith, once acquired, stays unshaken.

The sole purpose in the study of Vedanta is the realization of the Self; it is only incidentally concerned with the various attributes of the ego. One who has known one's own real Self can then realize the mighty Self who encompasses the universe. The dualists believe that the individual, the universe, and God are entirely separate units having their independent existences. By knowing their own selves they hope to acquire only a partial knowledge because according to them the Self is distinct from the universe and God. A wide gulf separates this school of thought from Vedanta. Vedanta helps us to go far beyond the concept of these separate entities. The most useful and elevating contribution of Vedanta is that God is not away from us, but dwells within us; he alone is the foundation of our individual existence. This is the central tenet in the philosophy of Vedanta.

CHAPTER 13

# *The Kingdom of God Is Within*

Having learned that God pervades the whole universe, that He is the Atman animating our soul, and that He is the life of our life, we should search for Him within us and not without. Our physical self is but an externalized manifestation of the Atman. The Atman is quite distinguishable from the physical self that moves, grows, decays, and finally dies. If we turn our eyes inward we will realize that the Atman alone is imperishable, while everything else perishes. One who cannot find Him within oneself can never find Him outside.

There are two methods of approach to self-knowledge. One is toward the gross, and the other is from gross to subtle. The first approach is not practicable. In the yoga of the *Kathopanishad* the aspirant goes to the deeper levels of being and finds the subtlest—Atman—the *summum bonum* of life. Vedanta philosophy leads the student to his innermost self. The Upanishads say, "The senses are beyond the body, and mind is beyond the senses. Intellect is beyond the mind, and far beyond is the kingdom of Atman." Here the word *beyond* means "within." As Atman is the innermost self, the aspirant should search for Atman within and not without.

An analysis of our sense perceptions and mental states helps us in entering into our inmost being. But before proceeding with such an analysis, the aspirant should first start probing into sense objects and his physical body. Our five senses are the main doors through which our individual ego comes into contact with the external world. These five senses are the gates through which we receive the vibrations from the external world. These vibrations are first carried into the brain cells. Molecular changes take place in these cells and the vibrations are in turn translated by the ego into sensations. Next, the sensations are formed into percepts, which after a series of mental processes are transformed into concepts. This goes on and on endlessly. To sum up, first we receive vibrations from external objects, then the vibrations are changed into appropriate sensations, the sensations in turn produce percepts, and the percepts are finally transformed into concepts. For instance, when you think of any object, you perceive instantaneously the mental image of that thing. It is called a concept.

Sound is nothing but the vibrations of air that enter through the ears and touch the organ of hearing, which produces vibrations in the auditory nerves, which in turn are carried into brain cells for producing certain requisite changes. These changes give rise to percepts, which are finally transformed into concepts by an intelligent mind. If an intelligent mind does not exist, there will be no perception. For instance, assuming that in an unconscious body the organs remain perfect, that the vibrations of air produce the necessary changes in the brain cells, there will still be sensation even with the absence of intelligence within. When we infer that a particular object is the cause of a sensation, we are able to find this object by tracing the cause of sensation or perception. It is not the sense organs that do the tracing, but the intelligent mind that performs the task.

In studying Vedanta, we must bring to bear on the subject at every stage a critical analysis and creative synthesis. For Vedanta is not merely the science of the Self, but also a system of philosophy. Vedanta describes the position thus: "Finer than the sense organs are the sensations, but the mind is beyond, and beyond the mind is the intellect, and greater than the intellect is the cosmic ego. Beyond the cosmic ego is the unmanifested one. This is the highest path that reaches the ultimate reality."

As we have seen, the sense organs are the gross instruments, and sensations are finer than these sense organs. The objects of perception in the external world are, on the other hand, grosser than our sense organs. Even sound and color are not higher or finer than the intelligent mind that reveals and enlightens them. A determinant is necessarily higher than the object to be determined.

Finer than sensation is the mind. Mind connotes the power of attention. One whose mind is not attentive when a sensation is produced cannot be aware of that sensation. For instance, you are sitting in your living room seeing all the things in it, but if your mind is far away, you will not see any of the objects in the living room. You are not conscious of them because you are not attentive. It is attention that reveals sensation. Without attention one cannot perceive any object of sensation. But mere attention alone is not sufficient to determine the nature of the sensation, whatever be its nature. Again, attention can be classified as voluntary or involuntary. Involuntary attention is not very useful. To develop voluntary attention is one of the purposes of the yoga of the *Kathopanishad,* without which concentration and meditation are not possible. The concentrated mind alone can help the aspirant in revealing the inner mysteries of life. Without the development of voluntary attention, the mind cannot be unfolded, and without the unfoldment of the mind the faculty of discrimination cannot be strengthened.

The power of discrimination is an entirely different faculty. The power that distinguishes one concept from another is called discrimination. This intellect, or the discriminative faculty, is exercised by the mind. There comes another higher and finer faculty, and that is the consciousness of "I" in the mind. This is called ego. The ego associates itself with sensations of one kind or another. The moment a person hears a sound he associates himself with that sensation, and this is how the sense of "I" binds all sensations, perceptions, and feelings. It is because of the ego that we feel pleasure and pain, and this particular faculty is subtler and finer than the other mental faculties. He who can sever the connection between sensations and the ego will have no feeling of pain or pleasure. It is thus that the practitioner of yoga avoids the pains and sorrows of the world. He conceives of himself as different from the body, separates himself from the body, and fixes his attention on something entirely different. He thus becomes immune to the feelings of pain and pleasure. The moment a yogi cuts off his connection with all the sensations of his sense organs, the external world simply does not exist in relation to him. The world exists only so long as it is linked to the ego.

When the yogi segregates the sense of "I" from the external world, he enters a state of nothingness, and the same "I," dispossessed of its feeling of "mine" and "thine," goes into the state of bliss, which is called *asamprajnata* (seedless) samadhi. It is the sense of "I" called the ego that divides us into separate and individual entities. Each and every individual ego is, as it were, an epicenter, which is called "I," and anything related to that center is "mine." That is the reason we usually do not display a keen interest in things that are not directly related to our ego. The sense of "I" unites all our sensations and molds our individual identity. For instance, it is through the sense of "I" that we are the same persons today that we were yesterday. However, although it is the creator of our identity, this sense of "I," or the ego, is not the ultimate reality. The sense of "I" also produces the sense of non-ego. If you think of "I am this," it also means that "I am not that." "I am this body" means, for example, "I am not that book." Every sense of "I" includes in itself the sense of "I am not," which is non-ego. The sense of "I" or the ego is the blending of two factors. The one is changeable, the other is unchangeable. The ego is thus a mixture of something changeable and something unchangeable.

The changeable something is the foundation of the phenomenal universe, of the body and its sense of external objects, and so on. It is the source of evolution. The universe has come into its present state by the process of evolutionary energy. The entire external world is nothing but the manifestation of force. When this force does not manifest itself in any form but remains dormant, it is called energy.

In modern science, also, solid matter has successively been reduced to empty atoms, then electrical particles, and then electromagnetic waves, which ultimately are shown to be forms of energy, and, in the last resort, to be mere ideas. No less a philosopher than Sir James Jeans believes that electrical and magnetic forces are mental constructs of our own, resulting from our misguided efforts to understand the motions of the particles. Another eminent scientist, Sir Arthur Eddington, says, "We must remember that the concept of substance has disappeared from fundamental physics and is replaced by a concept of the periodicity of waves. Modern science has indicated by experiment that the world of physics is a mental phenomenon. It is therefore no wonder that physics has virtually ended in metaphysics—thus confirming the intuitional revelations of ancient *rishis: Sarvam hi etad Brahma* (Verily all this is Brahman)."

The body and sense organs have come out of energy, they live by it, and ultimately go back into it. This energy is subject to evolution and is the source of our intellect. It has produced the intellect, the mind, and the sensory powers, which are but the different modes and forms of expression of energy. There is no intelligence in energy as such. If you are not conscious of energy, it does not exist in relation to you. It acquires force only when it is transformed into a state of consciousness. For instance, oil contains energy. When you burn it, it produces a fire and creates a force out of its energy. Thus, force becomes a form of energy only when consciousness gives it a form.

There are various states of consciousness, and we can also go beyond the phenomenal world. If we are not conscious of heat and cold, they do not exist so far as we are concerned. We can know of energy and force only when they become linked to our consciousness in some form or other. It must be remembered that the intelligent faculty in us is not a part of energy, but it is something distinct from energy. That which knows what is energy and what it is not, and that which stands beyond the undifferentiated energy, is called *Purusha,* the supreme Self, the absolute reality, the fountainhead of all consciousness and energy. Consciousness and energy produce the ego, and the absolute is the source and background of the entire Self and the universe. The difference between man and animal is that all the movements of animals are governed and controlled by nature while man is governed and controlled by ego. If the ego is purified, the "I"-consciousness leads the aspirant to consciousness of self. It is consciousness of self that should be cultivated. Cultivation of the consciousness of self is an inward art. Most of us remain in body consciousness and that is why we identify ourselves with the body. When the aspirant learns to separate the mortal self from the immortal self, the faculty of discrimination dawns. To have knowledge of the real and the unreal is the first step, according to the yoga of the *Kathopanishad*.

According to the philosophy of Vedanta, the ultimate reality is called Brahman, which is the final goal of the universe. It is said in the Vedas, "That from which the whole universe has come into existence, and in which it exists, and into which it returns at the time of dissolution, know that as the reality, that is your real Self." When a person knows this, all else will be revealed to him. By understanding his real Self, he knows the Self of all or the cosmic Self.

All knowledge comes from that one source, which is the highest reality. Intellectual knowledge is finite and mixed with ignorance. All sense perceptions are imperfect, and therefore unreliable. The source of all knowledge can be discovered only through Self-realization, which is man's supreme goal. One can achieve this goal by practicing yoga. Yoga is the instrument by which one can objectify oneself and study the real Self. Through yoga practices, one can achieve the power of introspection, throwing the light of intelligence inward within oneself. When the mental energy is withdrawn inward, inquiry into the realm of the subtle world can be commenced. Then and then only can one discover the eternal Atman and its relation to the supreme Self.

CHAPTER 14

# *The Human Body—Palace of Atman*

The King of Death compares the human body to the palace of a king, who is our Atman. The senses are the doors. There are eleven gates, and the sensory powers are the guards. The gates of the senses are our two eyes, two ears, two nostrils, mouth, navel, generating and excreting organs, and, finally, the *Brahmarandhra,* the gate leading to Brahman. This eleventh gate cannot ordinarily be known, as it opens only at the time of communion with the Atman in samadhi. It is called *Brahmarandhra,* "the seat of the Infinite." Atman is the king of the city of life. The king guides and directs all the attendants—mind, intellect, sense perceptions, and gross senses. Sensory powers are like door-keepers; they receive sensations and perceptions when we come into contact with external objects. These sensations and perceptions are presented as offerings to the great king, Atman, the ruler of this city of life.

Yogis serve this king by controlling their intellect, mind, and senses. Those who meditate constantly on the Atman merge with the Atman and are not born again. But those who do not attain that state will have to come back again to fulfill their worldly desires. There are those who believe that liberation is acquired in the life after death, but that is wrong. Perfection and liberation must be reached here in this life, and one who cannot reach it here in this life, cannot have it after death. Therefore, it is incumbent upon the aspirant to practice constant meditation, through which alone he can experience the Atman.

*Prana* and *vayu* are frequently used in the Upanishads as symbols of Brahman. The word *prana* means "first unit of energy in man." Man is a nucleus and the universe is its expansion. The prana that sustains life in the human body is the cause of the expansion of the universe. Anything that you observe and find in the phenomenal world is the manifestation of prana. The science of prana is vital, subtle, and deep. That is why the word *prana* has often been used in the Upanishads to refer to Brahman. The student should not be bewildered by such comparisons. Prana is identical with vayu, the wind, which is the vital breath of the universe. The words *prana* and *apana* frequently have been used for the two breaths—inhalation and exhalation. Actually the breaths are the vehicles for the pranas, and at times the word *vayu* has also been used in the same context. Prana is identical with vayu (energy), the vital breath of the universe. The breath of the individual is a practical manifestation of vayu, the cosmic breath. The body and the functioning of its organs is dependant on pranas. Even as the bees leave when the queen quits the hive and return when she returns, so thought, speech, and sensation follow the prana. As the spokes of the wheel hold to the hub, so do all these hold to prana. Devoid of the prana, a living being ceases to live. It is prana that maintains the life-link between the physical and mental sheaths.

Prana is not only the life principle in the individual, but it is also the cosmic principle. A variety of manas is attached to prana, such as breath, life, and the sense organs. Prana is the vital force in a living being that is incessantly active, whether one is awake or asleep. In deep sleep, the sense organs enter into the mind and the fires of the prana keep watch over them. According to its different functions, the prana is given five *names—prana, apana, vyana, udana,* and *samana*. The air which rises upward is prana, and that which moves downward is apana. Vyana sweeps like a flame through all the limbs. It sustains life when, for instance, in drawing a stiff bow an archer neither inhales nor exhales. Udana conducts the soul from the body at death, and by virtue of samana food is assimilated.

The five organs of action and the five organs of perception, the five pranas, the manas, and the buddhi constitute the subtle body, which accompanies the soul at the time of its rebirth. The gross body dissolves at death, but the subtle body departs. At the time of departure the body with the conscious mind are separated from their immortal part. The subconscious mind, which is the storehouse of merits and demerits, becomes the vehicle for the jiva, or soul. All the samskaras, or impressions, of our several lives remain in the storehouse of our subconscious mind in a latent state like seeds. The relation between the subtle body and the gross body is akin to that of the seed and the plant, for, as the seed contains all the qualities of the plant in its womb, so the subconscious mind retains all the samskaras of our previous lives.

According to Vedanta, the human body is divided into five sheaths or *koshas:* the gross, physical sheath *(annamaya sharira),* the sheath of prana *(pranamaya sharira)*, the sheath of mind *(manomaya sharira);* the sheath of intellect *(vijnanamaya sharira),* and the sheath of bliss *(anandamaya sharira)*. They are called sheaths because they cover the Atman as a sheath covers a sword. They are described as being formed of successive layers, one upon another. The physical sheath is the outermost and the sheath of bliss is the innermost. The Atman remains separate and detached from all these five sheaths. By cultivating unattachment, by progressively penetrating deeper and deeper, the aspirant finally realizes his Atman. These sheaths are the superimpositions that constitute the prison of ignorance for man; but when the true knowledge dawns, the fortress of ignorance crumbles, in the same manner that a house of cards falls with the touch of a finger.

There are three states of the soul—the waking state, the dream state, and the state of deep dreamless sleep. These three cover the totality of the soul's experiences in the relative world, while the Atman in its true nature as *turiya,* or the fourth state, is the detached witness of the soul's three states. During the state of deep sleep, the soul enjoys a freedom from all sufferings and pains, but in turiya it experiences itself completely detached from all its sheaths and states. Turiya, the superconscious state, has been termed, in Buddhist and Hindu scriptures, respectively, as nirvana and samadhi.

During the waking state, the Atman experiences the material world with all beings. It uses various sense organs as its instruments. There is no real difference between the waking and the dreaming states. In both states a false reality is contemplated and one's real Self remains quite unknown. The waking state, like the dreaming state, is a projection of maya, the world of many folds. The perceptions of the waking state are similar to those of the dreaming state. As the reality experienced by the dreamer is shattered on awakening, so too the reality of the waking state disappears during the dream state.

The dream state is a mental state of the dreamer, involving the subconscious mind. The experiences of the dream state look real so long as it lasts. On waking up from a dream we discover that this body and the senses were inactive and that, therefore, we were dreaming. The things that look very real in a dream are but mental images created by the mind without the help of the sense organs.

In deep sleep, when the dreamer passes into a profound slumber, he ceases dreaming. During such a slumber, the soul is united with the consciousness. The *Chandogya Upanishad* calls this state of Atman *sushupta;* that is, when a person sleeps, he is gone to his own self. The *Brihadaranyaka Upanishad* and the *Prashna Upanishad* also use the same terminology in describing the deep sleep state. There are no longer any objects of contact, there is no consciousness in the impartial sense. But this union is only apparent and is unlike the true union that follows the knowledge of the Atman. The sleeper returns to the consciousness of his waking state and becomes again his old self. In deep sleep, the Atman remains covered by a thin veil of ignorance. It is a state where there is no fear and where worldly desires lie quiescent. It is like the state of perfect communion with the Atman. Man does not know anything of the world within or without. In this state, a sinner and a saint are alike. But there is a vast difference between the state of deep sleep and that of samadhi, which is also called turiya. When a fool goes to sleep and wakes up, he still is a fool;

but when an aspirant attains the superconscious state, samadhi, he comes out as a sage. Samadhi is complete awareness of Atman, while in sleep there is no awareness at all.

In turiya, the fourth state, the Atman in its purest form is the illuminator. By the illumination of Atman, the aspirant is illuminated. The state of superconsciousness is the highest one to be achieved by the student of yoga. Deep sleep is a state in which one does not know what reality is. When the jiva that is asleep under the influence of maya is awakened, it then realizes its oneness within itself. Turiya is free from both the notion of the impersonal subject and the object; it pervades all the phenomena of the relative universe as the mirage pervades the desert. One whose ignorance is dispelled by meditation and discrimination realizes this state of turiya unrelated to the triple states of wakefulness, dream, and deep sleep.

## CHAPTER 15

# *The Doctrine of Rebirth*

From the most ancient time to the present day, the doctrine of rebirth of the soul has exercised a profound practical influence upon the people of the East. All the good and evil that befalls a person during a lifetime cannot be explained with any degree of certitude if we confine our attention to this life alone. What does one know of life who knows only one life? In the narrow span of a single life we cannot possibly reap the fruits of all our deeds. "A mortal ripens like corn and like corn he springs up again." But the seed is left. We are all born with blueprints of our lives, conditioned by the results of our past, and they determine our future.

Man is the architect of his own destiny. This reasoned belief makes the believer in the doctrine of rebirth accept responsibility for present pains and pleasures and gives him an opportunity to ensure for himself a happy future. As he learns to accept with equanimity his fortunes, pleasant and unpleasant, he can look forward to the future with joy and courage. If pains and sorrows are the results of past actions, then, in order to avoid suffering in his future existence, the wise man should desist from committing any more wrong deeds.

Through proper spiritual discipline, the yogis can easily learn about their past lives. The inward art of meditation is the only possible method for reaching the deeper levels of inner being. Once the conscious mind is controlled the subconscious mind remains to be dealt with. One who reaches the depth of the hidden portion of mind can know one's previous births easily. Some of the yogis avoid discussing the issue of past lives; but when the aspirant starts his inward search he has to face this reality because all the samskaras (impressions) that have remained dormant in seed form come forward for fulfillment. The conscious mind is only part of the mind, the mover of the activities of man. The conscious mind is a puppet in the hands of the subconscious mind. By studying only the puppet, no aspirant can know the mover, the main instrument, which remains in the background. In the stream of life, the mind is just like an iceberg and the little portion that floats above the surface of the water is called the conscious mind; but the vast portion remains hidden beneath the water. To know the Atman and the truth of rebirth, it is essential for the aspirant to study carefully that vast hidden portion of the mind; without knowing it, the doctrine of rebirth cannot be known.

The theory of rebirth cannot be proved by modern scientific methods. A scientific approach can only treat it as a plausible theory of life after death. The rishis of the Upanishads were not impressed by the theory of eternal retribution in heaven or hell, for this theory reveals a disproportionate relationship between cause and effect. Life on earth is short and bristles with temptations. Most of our wrong actions are due to faulty upbringing and uncongenial environment. To inflict upon the soul eternal punishment for the errors of a few years or even of a whole lifetime is to throw to the winds all sense of proportion. The ancient seers developed the doctrine of rebirth on a rational basis, showing that it is the desire for material objects that brings about a person's embodiment. Desires are of many kinds. Some are fulfilled through the human body, some in a sub-human body, and some in a super-human body. When a person has fulfilled all his desires through repeated births, and discovers that the relative world is held by the law of cause and effect, he longs for communion with Brahman, which alone is causeless. Unfulfilled desire is the cause of rebirth. Or, simply, desire is the mother of rebirth.

Western philosophers like Plato, Pythagoras, and Socrates

believed in the theory of rebirth and reincarnation. Nowhere in the Christian Bible and Zoroastrian scriptures has the doctrine of rebirth been explicitly mentioned. The reason is that during the period of Christ and Zoroaster it was a common belief. Nowhere in the scriptures has either prophet repudiated the belief.

Some religions deal extensively with the past and future, and some deal with life in the present. By dealing with the present, the future is saved. The good conduct of life that molds a person's life on this earth automatically directs the course of future life. Believing or not believing is not the important consideration. The fact is that if almighty God is kind and merciful and decides human destiny, there should not be any disparity in His creation. Equality is the law of the absolute, and disparity is man's making. According to the doctrine of rebirth, humans are fully responsible for their life here and hereafter.

The human body is the best instrument for the attainment of liberation from births and deaths, for, in a super-human body or in a sub-human body, one can experience only the results of one's past actions. Neither an angel nor an animal escapes from reaping the fruits of action, and, therefore, none can be liberated unless they are born again in a human body. According to the theory of rebirth, a soul is born again and again, depending on the merits or demerits of its actions, so that in every successive birth it may acquire more and more knowledge and in the end attain perfect liberation.

The theory of rebirth is in conformity with the law of cause and effect, which is the very basis of the physical universe. Rebirth is the inevitable corollary of the soul's indestructibility. The doctrine of rebirth belongs to *para-vidya,* "higher knowledge." This knowledge dispels the illusion of the individual soul and liberates it finally.

Each person is born into a world that has been fashioned by his own karmas of the past. Those who have realized the transient nature of life on earth or in heaven seek to avoid an endless repetition of births and deaths. Therefore, they aspire for *Brahma Loka,* the highest heaven from which one never returns. The teachings of the *Kathopanishad* begin with the direct question relating to the soul's hereafter. The teacher, the King of Death, in reply to Nachiketa, gives a discourse on the soul's indestructibility and then proceeds to state the doctrine of rebirth. "Some souls enter the ovum to be embodied as organic beings and some go into non-organic substance according to their work and knowledge," says the King of Death.

The Bhagavad Gita describes death as one of a series of changes. "Even as the embodied Self passes in this body through the stages of childhood, youth, and old age, so does it pass into another body. The realized souls are not bewildered by this." Rebirth is directly referred to in the following lines: "As a person casts off worn-out clothes and puts on those that are new, so the embodied Self casts off worn-out bodies and enters into others that are new."

When the soul, jiva, departs, it is followed by the vital energy, prana. And, when the prana departs, all the other organs follow. The soul with its particular consciousness goes into the body that is best suited to that consciousness. It is followed by knowledge, actions, and past experiences. It may confuse the aspirant, but after analyzing carefully the relationship between mind and body, he comes to know that it is breath that establishes the relationship between mind and body. The breathing system is the vehicle of the prana. When the inhalation and exhalation cease to function, there occurs what is called death; but with the help of subtle pranas all the former impressions or samskaras are preserved. Physical death is a change, no doubt, but it does not annihilate the existence of the subconscious mind and soul. The yogi remains fully aware of his departure. Just as a leech supported on a straw goes to the end and takes hold of another support by contracting itself, so does the Self throw this body aside to take hold of another support. As the goldsmith takes a little quantity of gold and fashions it into another better shape, so does the soul throw away this body and make another in a better form. Whatever the Self desires, it resolves; whatever it resolves, it works out; and whatever it works out, it attains.

**CHAPTER 16**

# *What Is Maya?*

The most ancient scriptures in the library of humankind today are the Vedas. The *Rig Veda* is the most ancient portion. The doctrine of maya can be traced to the *Rig Veda:* "Indra through maya assumes various forms." The *Rig Veda* speaks of two orders of experience. One is that of duality or multiplicity, which is known to us in our everyday life through the sense organs and sense perceptions. Multiplicity is impermanent and finite, with a beginning and an end. It is deprecated by the Vedic seers as the source of all grief and suffering. On the other hand, non-duality is everlasting, eternal, and immortal. It is identical with the absolute Reality *(sat),* Consciousness *(chit),* and Bliss *(ananda), satchitananda*. The attainment of non-duality is the *summum bonum* of spiritual evolution. Whatever reality the manifold phenomena possess is illusory, but non-duality is absolute and immutable.

Reality is one, but sages call it by various names. The diversity that we encounter in our daily life is maya, non-existent from the standpoint of ultimate Reality. The Upanishads declare that maya or empirical knowledge does not give true knowledge, but belongs to the realm of ignorance (avidya). Unreality, darkness, and death are duality and maya, whereas non-duality alone is Reality and immortality.

The *Ishopanishad* states that "The face of Truth is veiled with a golden disc." The veil must be removed so that the seeker may behold Truth. This veil or curtain has often been termed maya. But it must be understood that Brahman or the Atman is not to be sought on the other side of maya, nor is it to be realized after the veil is removed. Beyond maya there is no time. Nor is Brahman the cause of the universe, for Brahman is beyond the causal law. Brahman becomes real to us to such an extent that the universe with its time, space, and causal principle comes to be seen for what it really is—unreal. In other words, Brahman becomes real to the extent that we can shake off the illusion of the manifold world of appearances. The *Kathopanishad* teaches that the sages never find substance and certainty in the unrealities and uncertainties of the world. The *Mandukya Upanishad* states that when Brahman is realized, the fetters of the heart are broken and all doubts are dispelled.

The later commentators of Vedanta have developed the doctrine of maya in a more systematic manner. They tell us that if one accepts the concept of maya, one must also accept certain corollaries: namely, that the world is unreal, that life on earth is full of miseries, and that liberation consists in turning away from maya. Non-dualistic Vedanta depends upon the recognition of the two standpoints from which Truth can be observed. One is the relative standpoint and the other the absolute. The former regards time, space, and causation as actual, and, from that standpoint, the field of multiplicity as real. Good and evil exist, so also pleasure and pain. This world, on the other hand, is not real from the point of view of the Absolute. Duality disappears when the absolute Truth is known. The teaching of Vedanta illustrates the ultimate reality of Brahman. All that exists is Brahman.

The non-dualists describe creation as an illusory superimposition through the maya of names and forms upon Brahman. To illustrate this, they relate the story of a lion cub that was reared among a flock of sheep. The cub bleated and ate grass like the sheep. One day a forest lion pounced upon it and dragged it to a pond. There it was shown its reflection in the water, and a piece of meat was also pressed into its mouth. Then suddenly the veil dropped and the sheep-lion discovered himself to be a real lion.

In like manner, through the power of maya, or ignorance, names and forms are attributed to Brahman and in consequence the relative universe comes into existence. Through the negation of the illusory multiplicity, the true Reality becomes known. Brahman is not the least affected by the superimposition of illusory notions.

Relativity is maya. That the One appears as the many, the Absolute as the relative, the Infinite as the finite, is maya. The doctrine of maya accepts the reality of multiplicity only from the relative standpoint and contents itself with stating that the relationship of this relative reality with the Absolute cannot be described and known. In fact, there is no relationship between the One and the many, since there can be a relationship only between two existing entities. The One and the many do not, however, co-exist in the same sense. When anyone seeks to establish some kind of a relationship between the manifold universe and the non-dual Brahman, such a relationship is known as maya. A mirage is maya, and so also is its relationship with the desert. It is due to maya that one sees a rope as a snake, a mirage as water in the desert, and multiplicity in the place of the non-dual, indivisible Brahman. Vedantins agree that there is little difference between illusions, dreams, and experiences of the waking state: from the standpoint of the Absolute, they are all equally unreal.

The great non-dualistic sage Shankara describes maya as the power of the Absolute. It rests in Brahman and has no existence of its own. This relationship between Brahman and maya can be compared to the relationship between fire and its power of burning. Maya makes possible the appearance of a manifold universe and endorses names and forms of apparent reality. Yati Sadananda, another well-known non-dualist, defines maya as something positive though intangible, which cannot be explained as being or as non-being, which is made of three aspects (the three *gunas* of existence), and which is antagonistic to knowledge. The universe has a positive existence and cannot be called unreal, like the horns of a hare. It is seen to exist from the relative standpoint of Brahman.

Maya functions in the world through both the power of

concealment and the power of projection. The former, as in the case of a sleeping person, obscures the knowledge of the observer. It conceals, as it were, the true nature of Brahman. Conversely, the projecting power of maya creates the universe and all the objects seen in it, just as one begins to dream when one's consciousness is obscured by sleep. Actually, the two powers of maya function simultaneously. Therefore, Brahman in association with maya is called the creator or projector of the universe. *Maya, ajnana* (ignorance), *avidya* (illusion), and *prakriti* (the created universe) are all practically synonymous terms. Maya generally signifies the stupendous cosmic illusion on account of which Brahman appears as the creator, preserver, and destroyer of the universe. It is under the influence of ignorance that the Atman appears as the jiva, or the individual Self.

There are two ways of looking at maya: from the cosmic point of view, it is one; from the individual point of view, it is many. The cosmic maya is associated with Ishvara (Saguna Brahman, the Personal God), and forms its *upadhi,* or limiting superimposition. The individual maya limits the individual to "I"-consciousness and becomes its upadhi. Maya, both in its cosmic and individual aspects, merely hides the true nature of Brahman. Therefore the limitation is only apparent and not real. When the upadhi is discarded, the object formerly regarded as finite by the ignorant is realized as the infinite Brahman. Brahman uses this maya as the material of creation, that is, it creates the universe and its various objects out of maya. Maya has no independent existence of its own. Thus, maya is the material cause of the universe. But Brahman, as pure consciousness, is the efficient cause. This causal relation is often explained by the illustration of the spider and its web. When the spider wants to weave its web, it uses the filament that belongs to it, without which it cannot weave. The spider as a conscious creature is the efficient cause of the web, while the filament is the material cause. It must be remembered, however, that a causal relationship, in the usual sense of the term, cannot exist between the pure Brahman and the universe of names and forms.

The nature of Brahman or the Atman is Existence, Knowledge, and Bliss Absolute *(sat-chit-ananda)*. He is the one who dwells in our hearts. On account of maya, a person is not conscious of his real Self. The only way to liberation is to acquire knowledge of the Self. Atman is to be known here and now and not elsewhere after death. If a person knows the Atman here on this plane, he attains the true goal of life. If he does not know it here, a great destruction awaits him. Therefore, the Upanishads again and again lay down self-knowledge as the condition of Self-realization. Liberation is not something that is created, but is only a realization of that which exists through eternity, though concealed from us. All souls are by nature pure and free from all bondage. They are ever-illumined and liberated from the very beginning. People who do not know the location, the hidden center, fail to find it, though they walk over it again and again. Similarly, their souls, although going day after day into the world of Brahman, and although they are merged in Brahman even while asleep, still do not discover it because they are carried away by the ignorance of maya. He who knows Brahman verily becomes Brahman.

Desire is death and desirelessness is liberation. One who sees the whole universe in himself and himself in the universe cannot feel desire for anything. What can he crave for who has attained the source of all desires?

The knower of Brahman does not go to any realm, nor does the knower become anything other than what it has always been, that is, the pure Atman, the Self of all. Ignorant souls go to heaven or return to earth for the satisfaction of their unfulfilled desires. He who desires is born. But one who does not desire is not reborn. When all desires that dwell in the heart are erased, the aspirant becomes immortal and attains Brahman in this very body. The knower of the Atman is like a man who is awakened from sleep and dreams no more. He is like a man who, having been blind, receives back his sight. The knowledge of the Self liberates man from fear, desire, and death. There is one supreme ruler, the inmost Self of all beings, who is always awake. Eternal happiness belongs to the wise who perceive Him within.

A liberated soul, who has attained the blessed state of being free from doubt and whose knowledge of the Atman is not based upon mere intellect but upon the result of direct experience, whose illusion has been destroyed once and for all, does not come back. Such a one, a *jivanmukta,* is no longer concerned with bondage or liberation. Bondage and liberation are characteristics of the mind. On account of maya an ignorant person thinks of himself as bound and strives for liberation. As the person awakened from sleep does not reap the fruits of his dream actions, so the fully illumined person does not reap the fruits of his actions of the wakeful state. He sees action in non-action and non-action in action. Actions do not cling to him. He knows that the Self is not the doer but the witness.

The doctrine of maya has been explained explicitly by Shankara and his followers. The common person has no access to the lofty heights and ideals of the Advaita school of philosophy, but when the mind is cultivated and trained, made subtle and one-pointed, it is transformed and becomes a means for liberation. The purpose of all scriptural knowledge is to liberate the aspirant from the snares of maya.

Knowledge and meditation are the keys. Knowledge without *vairagya,* non-attachment, is of little use in attaining the highest state. The aspirant should gradually tread the path of controlling the senses. Then, making the mind one-pointed, he attains concentration. As concentration strengthens, meditation leads the student to the threshold of samadhi.

Without control of the sense organs and one-pointedness of mind, concentration and meditation are impossible. For mental concentration, all the activities—such as walking, touching, seeing, hearing, and so forth—must be brought under the aspirant's control. For if the sense organs remain active, the mind is attracted toward those activities, and one-pointedness is not achieved. While securing one-pointedness of mind, no physical act should be carried out by the practitioner. Even thinking should be eschewed. For if the thoughts keep on flowing in different directions, the mind cannot attain one-pointedness. The emotions—joy, grief, dejection, and so on—should not be allowed to intrude. There should not be any object in front of the practitioner that can cause emotional reactions. Concentration is impossible when the mind is prey to emotional strains.

Similarly, while one is under the influence of hunger and thirst there cannot be any mental concentration. When a person is extremely hungry, or has eaten too much, or feels sleepy after prolonged wakefulness, he can have no mental concentration. These obstructions to concentration can surely be removed if intense longing for concentration is there. When mental concentration is achieved, there arises a sense of profound satisfaction. This satisfaction that is derived from within cannot be achieved by any other means. It is, therefore, absolutely essential that the practitioner pay the most careful attention to one-pointedness of mind.

In the path of Self-realization the grace of God is the highest gift, which helps the aspirant in removing the innermost layer of ignorance. Ignorance or maya cannot be removed with the aspirant's efforts only. Divine grace comes after the aspirant establishes himself in *sadhana-sampatti,* or perfection. Sincerity, purity, faithfulness, and truthfulness are the virtues that help the aspirant in dispelling the darkness of maya and attaining the kingdom of the Atman.

CHAPTER 17

# The Cosmic Tree

The ultimate Reality is One, and beyond all appearances of names and forms. It cannot be illumined by the sun, the moon, or the stars. That same Reality is the root of phenomenal appearances. Here is an illustration. The universe is compared to the ashvattha tree, the holy fig tree that stands in a topsy-turvy condition: it has its roots upwards and its branches downwards. The essence of this tree is everlasting. The conception that the Vedic seers had regarding this universe is that it is eternal. It has come into existence from the infinite Reality that is One, and it will finally return to the same Reality. Unlike religious systems, Vedanta does not believe in the creation of the universe. It postulates the theory of cosmic evolution from that One which is the source of eternal energy. By comparing the universe with the ashvattha tree, one can get a clearer idea of the evolution of the universe. Just as we trace back the growth of the tree to its roots, the evolutionary process of the phenomenal universe has its start in the Infinite Being that is called Brahman. From that Infinite Substance everything has come into existence. The eternal energy, which may be called the mother of the universe, is *prakriti,* or creative nature. This energy is not separable from the infinite Reality; it is inseparable and one with the Reality. The sole cause of phenomena is Brahman, the infinite source of all intelligence and consciousness.

The illustration of the ashvattha tree is very apt, for although the ashvattha tree (the phenomenal world) in its essence is eternal, in its physical appearance it is but transitory. As far as appearances go, this world is constantly changing and transitory. All its forms and names are subject to continual mutation. We are growing every day and we are happy to notice this growth, forgetting for the moment that we grow older and older. We are not continually the same. It should not be forgotten that the tree of the phenomenal universe is subject to growth and change. Evolution means change. Everything in this world is subject to evolution and cannot remain stationary. All the experiences we have in this world, such as birth, growth, decay, and death, are going on and on endlessly. Everything that is perceptible, that can be seen or heard or touched or tasted, is changeable. Anyone who becomes attached to the gross material changing forms of the universe is sure to come to grief in the end. The wise therefore withdraw themselves from the gross and fix their gaze unwaveringly upon the finest Reality of the universe. In other words, those who can realize the root of the ashvattha tree, instead of being attracted by its flowers and fruits, are able to rise above all changes and reach the plane of immortality. It is thus that the King of Death describes the immortal and the mortal, the changeable and the unchangeable, by comparing the universe with the ashvattha tree. Those whose minds are deluded by various kinds of charms and attractions of the world cannot see the root, the infinite Reality of this universe. The true aspirant discovers this Reality, the root of the ashvattha tree, and he finally enters into the realm of immortality.

The word for "tree" in Sanskrit, *vrisksha,* is derived from its root, *vrisha,* which means "to cut": that which can be cut asunder is vriksha. Each and every individual is the center of the world wherein he dwells. By cutting off or renouncing the world, the realm of senses, perception, and desires is removed. The essence of this world, however, the seed of the ashvattha tree, is the inexplicable and the eternal *avyakta,* the unmanifested. The first manifestation of this seed is the breather of this universe. He produces and gradually develops Himself into a tree. The tree is only a gross form of the seed. The seed is not destroyed with the destruction of the gross form. The first manifestation of the cosmic Self arises from the Absolute Substance, and the eternal energy begins to evolve and manifest itself in the form of physical phenomena. This cosmic Self, according to Vedanta, is called Hiranyagarbha, the "one who dwells in the golden egg."

The Lord of the universe does not manifest Himself with any motive. As we go into deep sleep, our desires are latent and we do not have any duties. But when we wake up, all the latent desires again manifest themselves. Thus at the time of the dissolution of the universe, all souls are asleep in an undifferentiated state and their desires remain latent. The beginning of evolution serves to awaken this latent energy; that is, it causes the universe to begin functioning. Therefore, whatever exists in the macrocosm exists also in the microcosm.

We are not born out of nothing. We existed before, we exist now, and we will exist in the future, too. After the dissolution of the gross body, everything else remains latent. Our souls remain perfect and are not annihilated, dissolved, or destroyed after death. Death actually means change and not complete annihilation. The comparison of the phenomenal universe to the ashvattha tree is intended to convey the meaning that life is transitory and subject to change; everything in it will pass away. According to the Vedas, the Lord created the sun, moon, and stars after the pattern that existed in the previous cycle. In dissolution, all the forms and names of all the constituents of the universe disappear, but the Reality exists forever. The whole universe in dissolution is reduced to its subtlest form, which is eternal; its gross form alone is transitory. The King of Death, explaining the nature of the tree of the universe, has beautifully answered the question posed by the young seeker Nachiketa.

The King of Death further describes the cause of this phenomenal tree of the universe. All animate and inanimate objects of this universe are resultants of the vibration of *prana*. This vibration of prana is at the root of all universal phenomena and is the prime cause of all events happening in the universe.

Prana is the cosmic life-principle. It is that which makes us living beings; it is that which produces vibrations. Without vibrations and movements this world would not exist. Modern science has discovered that everything in this world is but the product of certain vibrations, which impel atoms to attract other atoms. Fire and electricity are but different states of vibration. When atoms and molecules vibrate in a particular direction, they produce electricity. All the external sensations such as color, sound, smell, taste, and touch are only vibrations. Our intellectual faculties are the result of vibrations. When we analyze a perception, we find that the rays of light that are constantly vibrating in a particular manner while contacting the retina produce an inverted image in the same way as in a camera. The pupil is like a lens, and the retina is like the plate on which the image is produced. That image produces certain vibrations in the optic nerves, which are then carried by the nerves into the brain cells, which in turn produce different vibrations. Similarly our breathing, our respiratory process, keeps all our organs in motion, and in consequence we have digestion and circulation of blood. We are able to live because every part of the immeasurable realm of prana is constantly vibrating.

So long as we are living in the darkness of ignorance we have the thought of "mine" and "thine," but we are in fact nothing but a mass of vibrations—a unit of energy of the infinite cosmic pranas. A wise person will never entertain this feeling of "I" and "mine." There is no such thing as loss or gain in this world of vibrations of prana. Even the body we possess, in which actions and reactions are constantly going on, is not ours. While ordinary people grieve over their losses, the wise person remains unaffected. He knows that whatever he possesses will not remain in his possession forever, and that he should not claim ownership of that which does not belong to him. Knowing this truth, he does not mourn over any loss. He knows that nothing is lost in this universe. He finds no *raison d'etre* for pains and sorrows, for although the body is liable to perish, the Atman is never destroyed.

The cosmic energy exists from eternity to eternity. The sun, moon, and stars and all other things of the universe come into existence from this very energy, and in the end they go back to the same eternal source. All that exists and happens in this universe is the result of motions and vibrations, the cause of which is the cosmic prana, which has its own laws. When it manifests itself in the internal world, it produces thoughts, desires, and emotions. Prana is thus the universal life. The first manifestation of this energy, this prana, was space, *akasha,* which gradually developed into this universe. The harmony that we see in the universe, in sun, moon, and stars, is rendered possible because everything in the universe owes its origin to the same source, namely, prana.

Intelligence and life go together. Wherever there is life, there is some manifestation of intelligence. According to Vedanta, there is no such thing as dead matter in this universe. The universe is a living organism. The electrons and protons contain motion; they are living. Where there is motion of any kind, there is manifestation of life, and therefore the whole universe is living. And if there is life in the universe, there must be intelligence in the universe. This universal force that breathes in the sacred heart of the universe is prana, the cosmic force, the ultimate mother of all forces. This prana is the cause of all the evolutionary processes. As a seed contains the power of growth, so does the seed of the universe contain the life force, the power of growth and evolution, in the latent state. When it begins to manifest itself, the cosmic evolution begins, the manifestation of the ashvattha tree of the universe begins. A human being is the finest product of this evolution.

The Ruler of Death explains that whatever exists in this phenomenal world is but the manifestation of the vibration of prana. According to the *Rig Veda* the cosmic force existed before the beginning of evolution: "At the time before the beginning of creation, there was neither existence nor non-existence. There was neither space nor time. Darkness ruled over darkness. There was neither death nor immortality. There was an eternal being who was breathing but breathless." *Breathless being* should be understood to mean the cosmic energy that produces breathing and causes motion and activity in the organs. From the one mighty source, all the forces of nature have burst into manifestation. The universe is the manifestation of that one who is the substratum of the universe.

All of us have come into existence by the power of prana.

The objective external world is only one half of the universe. What we perceive with our senses is not a complete world. The other half, which contains our mind, thoughts, and emotions, cannot be explained by the perception of external objects. For instance, if we try to find out the cause of our digestion of food, we must finally admit that there is some independent intelligence that actuates the process. Without the aid of this intelligence within, the mechanical processes of digestion cannot function. This intelligence is our inner Self, which possesses the prana, the life force. It is the Self that really lives and works with the help of this force.

By the power of prana and through the forces of evolution, the internal and external worlds come into existence. The whole world is eternal in its essential nature, but non-eternal in its external form. When all the forms of the universe are destroyed, the Formless Substance—the mother energy of the universe—will still live from eternity to eternity. Every object in this universe is obedient to the same mother energy. "That eternal universal life is a great terror. The sun, moon, and stars obey her and obey the law of prana." He who understands this truth finally realizes the mighty Self, transcends death, and becomes immortal. He who understands that infinite power under whose command all the planets are doing their duty, he who understands her laws, the laws by which we are governed, has known everything of the universe. So long as we remain in ignorance and think that we are one with the body and its gross and subtle forms, we have fear of death and remain under the sway of death. But one who realizes that he is formless has transcended death, has become deathless. The greatest obstacle in the path of realization is attachment to the body and to the external objects of the world. This attachment makes us slaves. Our wings are clipped: we cannot fly and soar high above in the infinite space of absolute Brahman. It is because of our attachment to sense objects that we experience fear of death and loss. But where is death or loss for one who has attained the formless Brahman-immortality?

The King of Death, having described the eternal nature of the great Brahman, gives a beautiful illustration: "From the terror of Brahman, the fire gets heat and light, the sun shines, the clouds rain, the wind blows, and death runs hither and thither." In fact, the fire, the sun, the wind, and the rain follow the laws of prana. They are the products of the forces governed by the laws of the Eternal. If that eternal infinite source is known before the dissolution of the body, one can reach the highest goal and become immortal. As the King of Death states: "One who has realized that the universal prana governs everything in the universe is free and liberated from the jaws of death."

CHAPTER 18

# Liberation—Here and Now

The King of Death explains, "One who realizes absolute Brahman in this life before dissolution of the physical self attains immortality, and one who cannot realize the highest truth, the real Self, will be born again on this plane." The Atman or real Self is to be realized in this very life, for it is not certain that we will get another opportunity to be born like this again. The human body is the finest in creation. Those who cannot make the best use of this human birth will remain under the bondage of the law of karma—cause and effect—and will not be able to transcend the laws that bind us to this plane. The attainment of Brahman is possible only here in this life and not after death. Those who have realized their real Self have become immortal. As we see our own face in a mirror clearly, so we can see our real Self in the cultivated and purified mirror of our intellect. Having acquired a human body on this plane, it is incumbent upon us to realize the highest Self. Those who believe that they can realize their real Self in the realm of the departed soul after death will be sadly disillusioned. Various pleasures of heaven hinder the soul from realizing the Atman. Also, there are different realms, lower and higher, in heaven.

Those who perform good deeds and lead righteous and selfless lives and have obtained some perfection in this life can enjoy a clear vision of the divine Self in the highest realm. But the wise say, "The highest attainment and realization of Self can be had only in this very life." Heavenly realms like *pitriloka* and *svargaloka* cannot reveal the highest truth. In pitriloka we meet our ancestors or the dear ones, and in svargaloka we enjoy various pleasures. But we cannot get liberation by going to such realms. Our longing for realization is to go higher and higher, and this longing will never cease until the highest goal is reached. When one is able to differentiate between transitory objects and the real Self, one will never remain satisfied with these intermediate planes and their pleasures.

No one has ever been fully satisfied with worldly pleasures and ambitions. The more we get, the more we want, and there is no end to it. Ambition causes dissatisfaction and it never brings happiness to man. The wise man realizes that the aim of life is to know his immortal Self. The body and mind are subject to change and it is truth alone that continues to remain unchanged. He who has realized his true Self has become immortal and has overcome all fears of death.

Fear of death proceeds from ignorance, from attachment to the body and its relations. The more we are attached, the greater is the fear we have, for we visualize a loss. But a wise man is always free from fear. He has no fear because he does not possess anything and he knows that the physical body is like a bubble in the ocean of infinity.

Our real Self is different. It is higher and eternal. One who can realize truth in this body attains Self-realization. Those who do not realize the immortal nature of their Atman before the dissolution of the body lose the great opportunity that comes as a result of human birth. A true aspirant does not crave worldly objects and prosperity. He sacrifices and withdraws his mind from worldly objects and realizes his true Self. He is a saint who has no attachment to worldly objects. He knows that he is the child of immortal bliss and is free from the bondages of the world. He who has realized this has attained divinity in this very life. In the *Kathopanishad* the King of Death elaborates on the truth that the Self, the Atman, is above and beyond mental and physical conditions.

According to the Upanishads, mind is superior to senses, intellect is superior to mind, and Hiranyagarbha, the cosmic Self, is superior to intellect. Realizing this, men cut asunder the vicious circle of birth and death and attain immortality. If we separate our real Self from sense perceptions and mental functions, we will recognize the Self as the unchanging eternal entity. All the pains and sorrows, pleasures and delights, are either on the sense plane or on the mental plane. The wise man is never affected by changes of body, senses, and mind. But he who has no knowledge and power of discrimination remains on the plane of senses and mind, and mistakes his non-Self as his real Self. The wise man with the help of his discriminative faculty knows that all the objects of this world are transitory and it is the Atman alone that is lasting.

Our real Self—the Atman, the immortal essence—remains hidden deep under several sheaths, physical and mental, gross and subtle. One who has no power of discrimination cannot understand the difference between the gross and the subtle, the non-Self and the Self. The faculty that is capable of distinguishing pain from pleasure, love from hatred, and other such mental functions, is called the intellect *(buddhi)*. The intellect is like a mirror that catches reflections of all the sense organs and perceptions and all thoughts and cognitions of the mind. The mind and the intellect are two different powers. The mind, which is a catalog of desires and emotions, is not the same as the intellect or the faculty of discrimination. The intellect is that power which discriminates and compares one thing with another.

The human intellect is a part of the cosmic intellect or cosmic ego. The cosmic ego is called Hiranyagarbha or Saguna Ishvara. He who wants to realize Brahman, which is beyond the cosmic ego, will have to go beyond Hiranyagarbha. Beyond cosmic ego is undifferentiated energy, which produces intellect and which is the mother of all. All the forces and powers of nature are potential in that undifferentiated state, even as energy remains potential in firewood. Only when firewood is burned do the flames shoot up. The energy that is then manifested in the form of fire was already there in firewood, but only in its potential state. Similarly, when the universe recedes into its primordial energy, it remains as a potential.

The tremendous energy that is radiating from the sun, moon, and stars remains latent in the mass of energy before the beginning of evolution. Electricity is taken from the atmosphere and stored in a powerhouse and distributed to different places. Even then it eventually goes back to its original source—the atmosphere. It is never discharged. In like manner there is neither gain nor loss in the process of evolution. Everything is conserved. Looking from the individual point of view, we may think that a particular manifestation gains or loses, just as firewood loses its energy when it is used. From the standpoint of universality, however, we find that nothing is lost or gained. In fact, the universe does not lose anything it already has, nor does it gain by any new addition.

The more we advance in realizing the grandeur of the universe and the eternal truth behind it, the less we worry about gains or losses. If all of humanity were to be destroyed, even then, from the metaphysical point of view, nothing would be destroyed. One who understands the eternal truth and the process of evolution will not grieve over any bereavements. Nature teaches us in our daily life by giving us kicks and blows, by snatching away our nearest and most beloved ones. She is telling us again and again to be detached because all the things on this plane belong to her. She says, "Wake up and claim not what does not belong to you."

Beyond the undifferentiated energy is the absolute Brahman, our real Self. One who can go beyond the realms of senses, mind, intellect, and ego can go to the kingdom of the immortal Self. The great thinkers of ancient times purified their hearts and minds and in the state of samadhi realized the highest Self. Their experiences are of universal value. They help the aspirant to rise above mundane matters and enter into the abode of infinite bliss—the Atman.

During samadhi the seers realized the highest reality. In their superconscious state everything was revealed to them. This state is beyond the reach of intellectual reasoning and faculties. The truth that is obtained through logical reasoning cannot be called revelation. Revelation issues from the superconscious state of samadhi. The seers of the Upanishads first realized the truth and only later sought the aid of logic to explain their revelation and make it intelligible to the ordinary person.

"The real Self cannot be perceived by the senses, for they cannot reveal it," says the King of Death. "The real Self cannot be seen face to face by the eye; the senses, mind, and intellect cannot reach there. It cannot be perceived by any of the senses. It can be realized only by the purified mind and heart." When the inner nature is purified of all its imperfections, the purified mind and heart can lead the intellect to have a glimpse of Atman. After this glimpse, the intellect and ego are transformed. These are transfigured into divine bliss. This can be done by intense *sadhana,* or yoga practice.

The sign of transfiguration is complete detachment from the body and worldly desires. A yogi strives always to be above attachments and desires. He gives up all the worldly pleasures and enjoyments and withdraws himself from all external conditions of life. When he realizes the blessed state of samadhi and his ego is transformed into divine bliss, the glory of the Atman shines upon his internal world. The grandeur of the Atman begins to dawn upon the horizon of the individual Self, and, with this divine glimpse, the yogi enters into the blissful realm of immortality and is finally liberated. One who has transcended all the universal laws of change cannot be held back by anything. Thus he realizes the ultimate goal of human life. Such realized saints can teach us how the ultimate goal can be attained.

The King of Death describes the state in which the realm of immortality is attained and the Atman is realized. He says, "When all senses are withdrawn from the organs and are silenced, when the mind is quiet and still and thoughts do not disturb the mind, in that state the glory of the Atman is realized and the bliss dawns upon the horizon. That is the state of samadhi. It is not a state of death. It is the sameness and oneness beyond the realms of the world—physical and mental. After tremendous storms and rains, there prevails an intense calmness. In like manner, after yoga practice or spiritual discipline, calmness prevails within and the bright sunshine of realization finally comes. "

The King of Death proceeds to describe how the highest state of samadhi can be attained. He says, "The state of samadhi or realization can be attained through the method of yoga discipline." Yoga means the method and process of concentration and meditation. Yoga is self-control. One who achieves a peaceful and well-balanced state of mind by withdrawing from worldly objects and by gaining self-control becomes a yogi. To practice yoga discipline requires strength and willpower to bring the senses, passions, and desires under control. Those who have neither a guide nor an intense longing for yoga practice cannot accomplish this control.

The aspirant who is well balanced and keeps his intellect, mind, and senses controlled and establishes harmony among thoughts, feelings, and deeds can attain the highest state of mental equilibrium. Self-control, however, does not mean that the aspirant becomes like a log of wood. It only means that all his senses and mental powers are controlled by transmitting them to a higher plane. Without self-control, the attainment of the highest Self is impossible. The first step of yoga is longing for the divine and the end of worldliness. Where worldliness ends, there the higher steps begin. The student of yoga steadfastly marches onward and does not stop until the goal is reached.

The King of Death describes the processes and methods of yoga discipline to the young seeker, Nachiketa. He says, "Neither by speech, nor by mind, nor by the power of sight can this realization be acquired." Yoga discipline leads to the supreme consciousness, which cannot be acquired by any other means and methods. The absolute reality is beyond physical and mental prowess; these cannot reveal the transcendental reality of the Atman. The reality is subtler than the subtlest and, therefore, the vehicle of words is quite insufficient to describe the blissful state of samadhi. It is beyond description because words are necessarily imperfect. Even certain higher feelings such as thoughts of love cannot be expressed through the language of the lips; they belong to the language of the heart. If it is difficult to express even ordinary love through words, it is certainly impossible to express the feeling of love for the Supreme Self. All the statements of different religions and faiths about the one Supreme Being appear contradictory and unsatisfactory because of the limitations of human speech to portray spiritual thoughts and experiences. What must be realized we cannot externally express. Thoughts and feelings cannot have any access whatsoever into the transcendental state of samadhi because it is a plane that is beyond thoughts and feelings. When all thoughts are purified and controlled, the aspirant, keeping his mind unalterable and one-pointed, crosses the bridge of ego and goes to the realm of the Atman.

Those who deny the existence of the Atman cannot realize Him. But those who have faith in their inner Self may realize Him and thus achieve final liberation. The Supreme Self is the cause of all, and yet it is causeless. It can be called the "causeless cause." It is beyond cause and effect, and nothing else exists that may be called the cause of the universe.

In order to attain the highest realization, the aspirant should develop God-consciousness and believe in the existence of God. The most valid proof is the proof of our own existence. If, however, we deny our own existence, we surely cannot find proof of the existence of God. To believe in the existence of the Self is the foundation of our consciousness of the existence of the Supreme. Had we come out of nothing, we would have remained nothing all the time, and then our end also would have amounted to nothingness. How can nothing create and manifest something? If we believe in our beginning and end as nothing, our present state is also nothing, and our endeavors and actions in the world are useless and an absolute waste of time. Those who believe in nothingness are like children playing with toys.

## CHAPTER 19

# *The Way of Yoga*

The explanation that Vedanta gives for the existence of the Self is remarkable for its rationality. During sleep we are not conscious of our bodies, but still we exist. We exist during the sleeping state not because of our bodies but by the fact of our own existence—the very existence that makes our bodies appear as existing. Materialistic thinkers declare that the soul exists because of the body and as a production of the body. In making this statement, they are putting the cart before the horse and cannot, therefore, arrive at any valid conclusions. It is not the body that produces the consciousness of existence. On the contrary, it is the consciousness of existence that keeps the body alive and activates it. That which moves our mind and body is our real Self. In fact, we know of the existence of others because we exist. Had we been non-existent, the sun, moon, stars, and the universe would not have existed. By denying self-existence, how can we know the existence of anything?

Says the King of Death, "When all desires and passions are removed, when perfect stillness prevails, the mortal becomes immortal." The yogi enters into the realm of immortality during his period of samadhi. It is very difficult indeed to go into that transcendental state, but it is not impossible. Yogis who go into samadhi are our real witnesses to this possibility, and even today many of them are found in the world. Inasmuch as the supreme Self is beyond speech, feeling, and thought and no evidence can be given for its existence, we can say nothing else but that He exists. One who really wants to ascertain His existence should be fully prepared to die and go to the abode of Death like the young seeker Nachiketa.

The King of Death instructs Nachiketa, "When all the knots of ignorance are destroyed in this very life, one enters the blissful kingdom of immortality." There are several knots (desires) of karma and an ordinary human life cannot destroy all of them. Life in this world of ignorance is very complex and filled with delusions and illusions as a result of maya, and it becomes very difficult indeed for one to separate the Self from non-Self.

The aspirant should purify his mind and heart by removing all the knots of desires, ambitions, and worldly passions. The knots of ignorance are real obstacles in the path of realization. Deluded mortals remain in the bondage of these knots and cannot destroy them. They are guided by such notions as "We are this," "We are that," and "We are happy" or "We are miserable," and so on. They are crazy for worldly things and they are always busy in satisfying their sensory desires.

In reality the physical self is the instrument of the Atman, and it is a valuable instrument in achieving Self-realization. But if it is used for fulfilling the demands of the physical self, we will only be groping in the darkness of ignorance. The truth is that we are the Atman and not the physical body. By mistaking the non-Self for the real Self, we go on committing mistakes and reaping the results of our actions. Whatever actions we have committed in the past produce their fruits in the present and future, and that is the real cause of our pains and sorrows. When the arrow is shot, it must go to its destination. So long as the arrow remains in our hands, we can choose its course. But once it is shot, it must take the course set for it. All the wrong deeds that we have committed in ignorance in our past produce their adverse effects. We should, therefore, be careful that we do not commit the same mistakes again.

When by the fire of knowledge and yoga practices all the knots of ignorance are destroyed, one becomes immortal. The

King of Death teaches that the moment an aspirant realizes his Atman by transcending the physical, mental, and intellectual realms, that very moment he becomes perfect and immortal. Young Nachiketa asks, "How can one become immortal? What will be the fate of those who cannot realize the Atman in this life or perform good deeds?"

The King of Death answers, "Those who cannot reach the highest state of yoga can gradually practice the performance of righteous deeds, and when they become conscious of their immortal nature, they will finally attain liberation." By the slow process of evolution, marching on toward higher and higher realms and crossing one after another, they finally reach the eternal kingdom of the Atman.

Describing the system of raja yoga, the King of Death says, "There are innumerable nerves and arteries and veins in the physical system, and among them the most important is that which goes upward through the spine. That one is called *sushumna*. It travels through the spinal column and leads to the highest heaven as conceived by the yogis. One who can enter sushumna at the time of death can attain Brahman, the highest goal of life. All other paths are paths of rebirths. From sushumna, the yogi ultimately reaches the highest consciousness of the Supreme Lord. By yogic practice, the yogi can commune with Parama Shiva, seated on the sacred throne of the thousand-petalled-lotus. Sushumna is the key point of liberation. From the *sahasrara* or crown chakra, he rises finally to the realm of the absolute Brahman.

When the yogi awakens the sleeping serpent power of *kundalini,* his consciousness enters into the path of sushumna. At the *ajna* chakra, the two-petalled lotus between the eyebrows, the yogi gathers the pranas and controls them at the time of death. He withdraws his mind completely from the lower plexuses (chakras). He withdraws all consciousness from the five lower plexuses and concentrates on the ajna chakra and then gradually upward toward sahasrara.

Human psychology and anatomy had been highly developed

during the Vedic period. The yogi who is well versed in these and who has complete command of his body and mind is fully self-controlled. By practicing yoga he knows how to die, and he also knows what will happen to him after death. It is such yogis who can lead the aspirant along the correct path. They can instruct us as to how the gross layer of the physical body can be removed so that the real Self can be attained. The scriptures can inform us what should be done but cannot reveal truth. Truth can be revealed only by him to whom it has already been revealed by the grace of the guru and God. Those whose minds are gross and attached to the material things of the world do not get the opportunity to meet such a master. We cannot force his appearance, and it may take years, even several generations, before we attain the fitness to meet him. Blessed indeed are they who have succeeded in this path, and fortunate are they who are treading it. It is not an easy path, but yet there is nothing greater and higher in life. One who has conquered the mind is the king of the self. The conqueror of worldly ambitions and desires is greater than the conquerors of the world throughout history. The essence of our being is immortal and deathless, and by following the path of yoga one can become immortal. The young seeker Nachiketa, realizing the immortal nature of Brahman, transcended the realm of thought and entered into the superconscious state of samadhi.

Before treading the path of yoga the aspirant should remember that he can succeed only if he keeps his mind pure and develops a sharp intellect and keen understanding. Only those who are able to withdraw their minds from the objects of distraction can concentrate on the Atman. Concentration of the mind is indispensable. Once Self is known, there is nothing else to be known.

The King of Death describes the process by which the aspirant can realize the true Self. He says, "Merge the words into thoughts." By words he means the power of speech. The words that are uttered by us are the expressions of our thoughts. No word is uttered without a thought behind it. In fact, words and thoughts are one and the same, but thoughts are finer and subtler, while words are gross. Similarly, all the external objects of the world are closely linked to the images that are in our minds. External objects can be brought back to their finer state of thoughts, the mind can be merged into the intellect, and when the power of discrimination is merged into the ego, we come to a point where all relationships with the external world cease to exist. Finally, the ego is merged into the real Self, the Atman. First, the aspirant withdraws his attention from the external objects, then from the body and the sense organs. Then comes the realm of subtler mental states and intellectual faculties. Lastly comes the ego, the sense of "I," "me," and "mine." Even when all other senses cease to function, there remains that constant sense of "I "—ego.

The real Self has no sense of "I." The Atman is undifferentiated and reposes in the state of pure bliss and silence. No words can reach it. The sun, moon, and stars are not to be seen there, for the Self is self-luminous and self-sufficient. The sun does not illumine it, but the sun is illumined by it. That self-luminous Self is our true Self. The limitations of time, space, and nature shrink away before its revelation. Death disappears before it like mist before the rising sun.

The King of Death describes the awakening of the soul, and instructs young seeker Nachiketa to learn the process by which the Atman is realized. He says, "It is possible only through the association and grace of the enlightened man, for the path is very difficult to tread. It is as dangerous as it is to walk on the sharp edge of a razor. The wise say that it is the most dangerous path. Those who cling to worldly attachments should not embark upon this venture at all. Before treading this path of yoga, the aspirant should rise above all attachments and attractions of the world. To reach the kingdom of the Atman, he will have to go step by step, beyond the realm of the senses, of the mind, and of the intellect. So long as one is circumscribed within the realm of thoughts, one is still on the plane of relativity, which is under the sway of constant change and death. The nets of death are spread up to the realm of the ego, but beyond that is the kingdom of bliss and eternity where death has no access. That eternal blissful reality is beyond the realms of sound, color, and the lights of the sun, moon, and stars.

Those who are fascinated by external sounds and colors are only deluding themselves. Vedanta tells us to rise above self-delusion and see things as they are in reality.

Is there anything worth possessing in this world? We will have to leave our beloved body and everything connected with the body, when we depart. Nothing can be claimed as our own in this phenomenal world. Such an imperfect world cannot give us permanent happiness. We try in vain and proclaim that we are improving the social conditions of the world in which we live. But we are only muddling things up because of our own ignorance and imperfections. The genuine student of yoga sets out to win immortal bliss and remains poised to face death at any moment, for he is convinced that he cannot die and that his real Self is deathless. The pursuit of material things takes away all the strength from us. One who can rise higher and realize the glory and majesty of the Atman is free from all sorrows.

The wise person, the seeker of truth, never craves and prays for material things, for he knows that they are only hindrances in the path of realization. He is firm in his conviction that our immortal life is beginningless and endless. After answering all questions of Nachiketa, the King of Death puts the entire philosophy in a nutshell when he enjoins upon his disciple, "Know that Atman." He who has known that immortal Self has himself become immortal: "Knowing is being." One who has known the immortal Self becomes immortal. When one knows God, one is God-conscious in every breath of life. True love permeates that exalted state of God-consciousness. It is never based upon selfishness. True love is based on wisdom, bliss, and knowledge. In the highest sense, true love and knowledge are one and the same. In ordinary mortals, selfish love predominates, while the love for the divine is only a secondary matter.

The story of Nachiketa and the injunctions given by the King of Death will bring enlightenment to those who listen to it attentively. Those who study the story of Nachiketa under a realized guru will attain everlasting glory and bliss. Finally they go to the kingdom of the Atman and are liberated. The secret that has been revealed by the King of Death is the greatest of all secrets for every human being who wishes to know where he will live after death. For ordinary mortals this remains a secret for many births to come. The fortunate aspirant who receives enlightenment at the hands of a realized guru grasps the mystery of death very clearly and to his fullest satisfaction.

The King of Death finally liberated Nachiketa from the sway of death and rebirth. He who discovers the great secret of the *Kathopanishad* should be able to liberate himself like Nachiketa, provided he is prepared to go to the abode of Death with mind and heart purified and ready for Self-realization.

**APPENDIX A**

# *Signs of Impending Death*

The mysteries of life and death and life hereafter are known to a fortunate few only. Death is but a comma and not a full stop. Death is a solemn experience, a change from which none can escape. One who does not prepare for it is a fool.

The materialist finds it difficult to believe that anything continues to exist after death. He cannot catch the glimpse of the beyond because he lives on sense perceptions only. The Buddhists and the yogis believe in and discriminate between the soul, the mind, and the body.

The soul is uncreated, is essentially consciousness, and is perfect. After the physical death it is the soul that survives. If the soul is the real entity and existence, there should be some way to experience it.

According to the Buddhists and the yogis, there are certain psychological methods by which the experience of the Self can be obtained. Every aspirant can have this experience, provided he undertakes the appropriate spiritual discipline.

An aspirant, by living a life according to spiritual instructions, first purifies his mind and then renounces all attachments, charms, and temptations for worldly values and thus becomes capable of knowing the true nature of Self. He passes beyond the operation of karma. He attains *amrit tattva,* or immortality.

Death is capable of destroying flowers but is unable to harm the seeds. Birth and death are two noble expressions. Wise is he who renounces the world of fragments, that he may enjoy the world wholly and without interruptions. Death is a strong force that forges the chain of cruelties in life with an enduring justice. Death is stronger than life, but single-minded love for God is stronger than death. Life and death are only different names for he same fact—the two sides of a coin. Death rounds off life's tragedies and makes life beautiful. One who goes beyond differentiation can conquer death and reach the other shore of eternal life.

The Atman never changes, never goes anywhere, and never returns. It is the eternal witness of all. The universe is its manifestation, without beginning and end, ever going on.

The reality of life is life itself, whose beginning is not in the womb and whose ending is not with the grave, for the years that pass are naught but a moment of eternal life, and the world of matter and its forms is but a dream compared to the awakening that we call the terror of death. The fullness of life is the attainment of spiritual blessedness, from which there is no fall into a life of ignorance again. Life after death can be experienced here in this very life by those who have attained samadhi. There are various states, and the highest state of samadhi can be realized, but it is inexplicable.

Certain signs and symptoms of death explained in the yogic scriptures are presented here to the aspirants for experiment and verification. I have been verifying these signs and symptoms by noting actual cases, and almost all of the symptoms have proved true. Some significant signs of death forecast their shadows to a person whose death is near. Any student of yoga can easily know the approach of death by the signs mentioned below.

1. It is stated in the *Kathopanishad, "Angushtha-matrah purushah;"* that is, "The soul is the size of a thumb"—a pure, illumined, smokeless flame *(purusha),* which is seated in the center of the city of the heart. The fountainhead of energy, which is the central link between the upper and lower hemispheres, is called the *anahata* chakra. This inner center is very important to be known. There is a connection

between this center and the actual thumbs of the body, for it has been observed that a few hours before a person dies, the thumbs of both hands get very loose and drop down and cannot be lifted by the dying one. The dying person cannot move his thumbs in a normal way. It is certain that such a person will die within three days.

2. One cannot see his own head when viewing one's face in the mirror. All human figures and objects of the world become hazy and cloudy. One gradually loses the power of sight. Such a person is sure to die within ten days.
3. The person who sees two moons in the sky will die within three months.
4. If one perceives a hole in his shadow, it is presumed that one will die within a month.
5. After shutting the ears, if a person does not hear the sound of the pranas, and an irregular heartbeat continues, he will die within seven days.
6. When a person sees a tree of a golden color, he will die in fifteen days.
7. If a person does not see and feel his lower limbs, it is certain that he cannot survive and will die within five days.
8. When one embraces a dead man in a dream, one will survive only for six months.
9. He who sees himself worried and sitting naked, while flowing tears for the departed one in a dream, will survive only for twenty-one days.
10. If a person's body suddenly becomes abnormally fat, he may die within six months.
11. If a person perceives a hole in the sun and the moon, his death is imminent.
12. If a person does not see the tip of his tongue, he will live only for three days.
13. When a miser suddenly becomes charitable and a charitable person a miser, these sudden changes are significant, indicating the major change called death. Such a person dies within six months.

There are several other signs, and so far as I have noticed, the dropping of the thumbs is a sure sign of death. After perceiving and noticing such signs and symptoms of death, the students of yoga do not start mourning their death or leave their meditation. They engage themselves intensely with meditation.

A time comes when none can help us. There is an intermediate state between life and death. It is a state when prana ceases functioning. If the student of yoga does not prepare himself for this moment, he suffers mental tortures and cannot explain or express himself to others. But if he has known the Reality, he will be saved from that calamity.

My presentation of the signs of death is based on my personal experience as well as on the experience of yogis whom I have met. I met a yogi in Sikkim State at Paidung in the year 1947. He could die according to his will and could give life to the dead. He demonstrated this feat more than five times. During those days I was anxious to know this mystery, termed *parakaya pravesha*. The yogi asked me to bring a living ant and I personally cut it with a sharp blade into three parts and scattered them at a distance of ten feet. The yogi suddenly went into deep meditation. We examined his pulse, heartbeat, and breath; but there was no sign of life. Before he reached the state of deep meditation, there were violent jerks in his body.

The scattered parts of the ant moved together and united in a second's time. The ant came to life and started crawling. We kept it under observation for three days. The yogi explained two methods of bringing the dead into life—one through solar science and the other through *prana vidya* (the science of prana). Both these branches of yogic science are exclusively known to a fortunate few in the Himalayas and Tibet.

One more interesting instance I would like to mention here regards a death predicted by a yogi during *Kumbha Mela* in 1966 at Allahabad. One of my friends, Vinaya Maharaj, sent a messenger to my camp informing me that I should go and witness his death. On *Vasanta Panchami* morning, at 4:30 a.m., he left his body before us, saying, "Please witness my death." We remained talking up to 4:28 a.m. on yoga and Vedanta and suddenly he said, "Now the time has come." He applied *siddhasana* and left his body smilingly. We all took our bath and dipped him in the Ganges at Sangam. It may appear fantastic to the readers, but the actual practitioners of yoga are accustomed to such experiences.

I found a lady who used to practice nada yoga at Kanpur. She was the mother of a famous doctor, G. N. Tandon, and she also had her death in samadhi before us. She was a fine person throughout her life, and during her last days she was completely detached and merged in her *sadhana* (spiritual practices). She left her body in complete consciousness. Hundreds of people witnessed the holy death of this lady saint who lived a householder's life. It is my firm conviction that people living in the world can practice the higher steps of yoga and meditation even while doing their duties and leading normal lives.

In the year 1938, when I was sent to Benaras to stay with a Bengali couple, I was informed that the couple would leave their bodies together. The couple had been meditating together for several years. They announced their death date and I was one of the witnesses. During those days, I sought to understand this mystery, which took me in search of yogis in the valleys of the Himalayas, and to Assam, Sikkim, and Tibet. These real yogis of the highest order are still not known publicly. After treading this path I am fully convinced that yoga is not meant to gain worldly achievements but to accomplish the union of jiva and Shiva within.

**APPENDIX B**

# *The Path of Yoga*

Yoga means unification, the union of jiva (the individual soul) with Brahman. There are various aspects of yoga, any one of which may be chosen according to the attitude and temperament of the aspirant. Yoga in its general sense includes karma yoga, bhakti yoga, jnana yoga, laya yoga, hatha yoga, and raja yoga. There is a popular misconception that hatha yoga is the only form of yoga. Hatha is the union between *ha* and *tha—ha* means sun and *tha* means moon. *Prana* is one of the names of the sun and *apana* is a name of the moon. Thus hatha connotes a union between prana and apana. Hatha yoga prepares the student for raja yoga and is ancillary to it.

Yoga is an exact science. It is a complete system through which one can acquire a total mastery over one's entire nature, provided it is practiced under the guidance of a competent guru and not through book knowledge. It helps the student to attain perfect concentration of mind and to uncover hidden mental and physical potentials. It is a system that helps the student to enter into conscious communion with the Lord of the heart and life and to attain final liberation. The highest steps of yoga doubtless transmute the practitioner into a divine personality. Yoga is a master key to reopen the sacred realms of eternal bliss and peace. It is concerned with the control of mind and body. The mind-stuff reflects the apparent existence of the phenomenal world, and its neutralization eventually leads the yogic practitioner to the highest goal.

Patanjali in his yoga aphorisms defines yoga as *"Yogash chitta-vritti-nirodhah"* (sutra 1.2), which implies preventing the mind-stuff *(chitta)* from taking various forms *(vritti)*. This mind-stuff is correlated with the mind *(manas),* intelligence or the determinative faculty *(buddhi),* and egoism *(ahankara),* which four together form the internal instruments *(antah-karana-chatushtaya)*. They are but various processes in the mind-stuff, or chitta. The waves of thought in the chitta are called vrittis. From the infinite storehouse of nature, the instrument called chitta takes hold of some reality, absorbs it, and expresses it as thought. The calm person is he who has control over his mind's waves.

## Essential Preliminaries

*Yama, niyama, asana, pranayama, pratyahara, dharana, dhyana,* and *samadhi* are the eight steps in raja yoga, which is also called *ashtanga* yoga. The five yamas, or great vows—consisting of non-injury *(ahimsa),* truth *(satya),* non-covetousness *(asteya),* chastity in thought, word, and deed *(brahmacharya),* not receiving any present from anyone *(aparigraha)—and* the five niyamas, or regular habits and observances—consisting of austerity *(tapas),* self-study *(svadhyaya),* contentment *(santosha),* purity *(shaucha).* and reliance upon God *(Ishvara-pranidhana)* are the essential preliminaries for any aspirant of yoga, without which any attempt in the direction of yoga disciplines is bound to be a failure.

## Steady Posture

After having equipped himself with a favorable mental background, the next formal step for an aspirant of yoga is the posture (asana). The student of yoga should keep his trunk, neck, and head in a straight line, and the body should be made steady and absolutely motionless. None of the limbs should move and the body must remain free from any disturbance. Only breathing and the beating of the heart continue. Breath, too, can be controlled for some time, but the practitioner has no sway over the activity of his heart. His attitude toward the body should make him feel as though it is not his own. Such a state is called the even state, when the vital energy *(majja)* flows through the spine uninterruptedly. The flow goes on from the head to the lowest part of the spine. There are two currents in this, the positive and the negative. The even flow is maintained through the middle *nadi,* or subtle nerve channel. The faultlessness of the entire nervous system depends upon the uninterrupted state of this flow. The natural delight available as a result of perfection in meditation can be secured by this steady posture. The student should consider *padmasana, siddhasana, swastikasana,* and *sukhasana** and select the one meditation posture that is suitable for himself. The spinal cord, although not attached to the vertebral column, is yet inside of it, and if the student sits crookedly, he disturbs the spinal cord. To achieve meditation, the three parts of the body—the chest, the neck, and the head—must always be held straight in one line.

## Breath Control

After having acquired a steady posture, the second step is controlling the nerves through pranayama. *Prana* means the vital force and *yama* means controlling it. In the initial stages one should try to purify his nerves *(nadi shodhanam)* by breathing deeply in a measured way, in and out, which will help in harmonizing the system. After practicing in this way for some months, one should, with the guidance of a guru, undertake pranayama by filling the lungs with breath through the left nostril *(ida),* holding it, and then expelling it through the right nostril *(pingala).* This makes one pranayama, which consists of three parts—filling *(puraka),* restraining *(kumbhaka),* and emptying *(rechaka).* In the beginning, the timing of each process should be according to one's capacity, and slowly, by gradual practice, it should be increased. It may be done daily four times or more, both in the morning and evening.

* For a description of these postures see chapter 3 of *Meditation and its Practice* by Swami Rama, a Himalayan Institute publication.

## Control of Senses

The next step is pratyahara, which consists in bringing the organs of sense *(indriyas)* under the control of the will. The indriyas always have a tendency to act outwardly and come in contact with external objects. The persistent tendency of the mind is to exploit the senses without control. In the first few months of practice, one may feel frustrated, but constant effort will tame the dissipation of the mind. Gradually the mind will be amenable to control. Only after a patient and continuous struggle can the attempt in this direction succeed.

## Concentration

Concentration (dharana) is fixing the mind on an external object or an internal point. There cannot be concentration without something upon which the mind may rest. In the beginning the senses draw the aspirant out and perturb his peace of mind. One should learn to pacify the bubbling thoughts and calm the emotions. Enormous patience and untiring perseverence are absolutely essential. Laziness and other adverse forces divert the aspirant away from his path.

All of us possess the ability of concentration in varying degrees. This ability should be systematically developed to the highest possible extent. Mere wrestling with the mind will not bring the desired results. One whose mind and heart are filled with fierce passions and fantastic desires can hardly concentrate on any object for long. Purity of mind and heart along with intense longing is very necessary before treading this path. Disciplining the senses, annihilating lust, greed, and anger, serves to increase the power of concentration. A person of concentration easily gets the penetrative insight, but mere concentration without purity is of no use in the path of yoga.

The student of yoga who by practice has acquired a steady posture and has purified his nerves as well as his mind by constant practice of breath control will be able to concentrate easily. Purification of nerves is indispensable before ascending the higher steps; success in concentration may then be obtained within a period of three months. Often, impatient aspirants take to intense concentration without having sufficient knowledge of the practice of even the rudimentary steps. Without a preliminary knowledge of yoga and its spiritual disciplines, the aspirant will not develop the power of attention for good concentration and meditation. One should be meticulously careful in laying a foundation composed of right conduct, correct postures, regulation of breath, and withdrawal of senses from objects.

Without the control of the sense organs, one-pointedness of mind is impossible. If the sense organs on their own accord try to be active, the mind will be attracted toward those activities, and one-pointedness will not be achieved. While practicing one-pointedness of mind, no physical act should be carried out. Even thinking should be eschewed. The emotions of joy, grief, or dejection should not be allowed to intrude. There should not be any object in front of the practitioner to cause an emotional reaction, for concentration is impossible when the mind is susceptible to emotional stimulation.

Similarly, while under the influence of hunger and thirst, there cannot be any mental concentration. When a person is extremely hungry or has eaten too much or feels sleepy after prolonged wakefulness, he can have no mental concentration. These are several of the distractions to concentration, which can be removed if there is intense longing. When, however, mental concentration is achieved, there arises a sense of profound satisfaction. A satisfaction that is derived from within cannot be equalled by any other means. It is, therefore, absolutely essential that the aspirant should carefully attend to one-pointedness of mind.

In the beginning, the mind should have an object to rest upon—a fixed object that is pleasing. Concentration is rendered very difficult indeed when the mind focuses on an object that it dislikes. Here, a competent teacher is necessary, to advise the student about the possible objects and desires of the mind. While the mind retains a tendency to brood negatively, concentration confers on the aspirant the qualities of accuracy and efficiency. The person who has acquired concentration does his job better and quicker. In addition, concentration quells wandering thoughts and emotional impediments; helps in securing worldly success; and clears cloudy and hazy ideas, bringing them under a correct perspective. The toughest tasks are facilitated for the person who practices systematic concentration

## Meditation

Meditation (dhyana) helps the aspirant of yoga to elevate himself to the higher realms of eternal bliss and everlasting peace. The mysterious ladder of yoga connects the gross and the subtle. It takes the aspirant finally to the immortal abode of Brahman beyond all the gross and subtle realms. Concentration flows into meditation like the continuous flow of oil from one vessel to another, meditation being the continuous flow of one thought. The best times for practicing meditation are from 3:00 to 6:00 a.m. and 5:00 to 8:00 p.m. The advanced students may practice meditation at midnight, when the atmosphere is very calm and quiet.

While there are several methods of meditation, they fall under two broad categories: the first, with attributes, and the second, without attributes. They are called concrete meditation and abstract meditation, respectively. In concrete meditation, the student meditates on forms such as a deity or a guru. In abstract meditation, he meditates on *pranava (Aum)* or the Atman, which is beyond the body, senses, mind, intellect, and ego. During meditation one should not allow access to any object other than that which is being meditated upon. Meditation on Aum, the eternal sound, with its meaning and feeling, is one of the best ways of controlling the mind. It is called *nirguna* dhyana. No other thought except the repetition of Aum without any break should be allowed. After practicing this for some time, the practitioner gradually develops the habit of abstracting the mind from the senses and their objects. When the mind remains in itself and realizes its superconscious state—a silent state of bliss—then the practitioner experiences a surge of joy and an intensification of meditation.

The aspirant should possess full determination and should keep his mind continually informed that he is pure consciousness, distinct from the body, mind, prana, and the senses. After some time, the aspirant achieves cheerfulness, contentment, and unruffled patience. There are certain signs of progress in the path of meditation, just as there are milestones on the road, and one who practices knows where he is and how far he has to go. With progress in meditation, all desires and passions melt away of their own accord. The senses and the mind become controlled and calm. Once the aspirant tastes even a grain of deep meditation, he will cease to be attracted by the fleeting pleasures of the world. The aspirant will become quite proficient in discriminating between sensual pleasures and spiritual bliss.

Meditation on the Atman is indisputably higher than any other object. The Atman dwells within the cavity of the heart. The yogic heart is not the physical heart that can be reached by the surgeon's knife. It is not a lump of flesh but a focal point that governs the entire system of life and light. It is the spiritual heart. It is the focal center *(anahata* chakra) that connects the three lower plexuses—that is, the inner centers *(muladhara* chakra, *swadhisthana* chakra, *manipura* chakra)—with the three upper plexuses *(vishudha* chakra, *ajna* chakra, *sahasrara* chakra). The physical heart governs only the physical self, by supplying blood to the body and through it to the brain. We have, in fact, three bodies: the gross, the subtle, and the subtlest. The spiritual heart on which the yogis contemplate is located within the cavity of the physical heart but is quite invisible to the senses and the mind. For more precise knowledge on the matter, the reader should approach yogis who have trodden this path, for this is a highly advanced process that is only orally taught by the guru to his disciples in secret. One cannot tread this path unless one is animated by an unquenchable desire to know this secret, mysterious ladder of yoga. When the disciple is ready, the guru appears. When the student is sincere, he certainly gets divine help.

Those who practice meditation regularly and systematically as instructed by the teacher get into the mood of meditation easily. The more one meditates, the more one gets the power of penetration or one-pointedness of mind, and finally the power of introspection. At this stage of introspection, the mind and the senses do not play their customary tricks, and sensory objects lose their power of attraction. With the mind fully illumined, the veil of ignorance drops. All worldly ideas and sheaths dissolve. All differences and distinctions disappear in the final state of meditation, samadhi. In samadhi there is the union of the human and the divine, the jiva and Brahman. Samadhi is absolute oneness. It is the summit of raja yoga.

## Samadhi

The path described by the King of Death in the *Katho-panishad* is the path of yoga, whose aim is the spiritual union between the individual soul and the supreme Self, between the soul and Brahman. Hatha yoga, as a course of psychophysiological discipline, aids in ascending the higher rungs of the yoga ladder. Through the discipline of hatha yoga, the attainment of complete mastery over the physical self and the nervous system can be achieved. It is regrettable that, in what is now technically called hatha yoga, neither the whole nor even the best part of it is practiced. In its true sense, hatha yoga is practiced for making the psychophysical organism perfectly fit for the highest steps of raja yoga. In all systems of yoga, control of mind, purity of heart, and physical fitness are demanded of the practitioner.

The ultimate aim of raja yoga is to lead the student to its highest rung: samadhi. There are two kinds of samadhi: *savikalpa* (with form) and *nirvikalpa* (without form). "I am witness to the various states of the mind, which are continually appearing and disappearing, and I perceive the objects of this mental marketplace indifferently"—this is called the phenomenal or savikalpa samadhi. During this state, the yogi looks on worldly objects like an indifferent wayfarer whose eyes do not take in the topography along the road. He looks at his own physical and mental states and processes as though they do not belong to him. Even as a juggler is not deceived by the visions he creates, so the yogi, who does not consider his physical and mental states as his own, is not deceived by them. He remains completely detached, secure in his realization that he is different from them. This is called savikalpa samadhi, because the thinker, the object, and the means (thinking) are all present during this state.

There is another state that is called *asamprajnata* or *nirvikalpa* samadhi. In this state, one is free from all attachments and is self-existent, self-evident, and peaceful. To remain rooted to the "there-is-no-duality-in-me-and-only-I-exist" state is nirvikalpa samadhi. In this deeper state, the means and the objects of thought do not exist; only the knower himself exists. It is the culmination of the former state. Nirvikalpa is the highest state, in which the yogi merges himself with the bliss eternal and expands self-identity into the "I-alone-exist" state, wherein he rests in complete peace, in union with his real Self, the Atman. It is a state of oneness and sameness that cannot be explained fully by the written word.

The difference between samadhi and deep sleep is seemingly very little. It can be illustrated this way: two men go to see a king. The first man sleeps while the other man remains awake. The one who is awake is in samadhi. Of course, the one who sleeps is also before the king, but is not aware of the king's presence. Deep sleep is a state of joy, but one is not aware of it. In samadhi, the yogi is fully aware of his blissful state. It is direct experience, which he derives from his Atman, and it cannot be fathomed through any other means. The experience of samadhi cannot be explained, for it is a unique state beyond thought, word, and deed. When the bee gets into the petals of the lotus and sits over the fountainhead of the nectar, how can it describe its joy while drinking it? Human life is bound by innumerable bondages. He who discards them, one after the other, some day reaches the kingdom of Atman. When samadhi is achieved, the aspirant is free forever. This is the highest stage of raja yoga, the permanent abode of deathless yogis.

# About Swami Rama

ONE OF THE greatest adepts, teachers, writers, and humanitarians of the 20th century, Swami Rama is the founder of the Himalayan Institute. Born in the Himalayas, he was raised from early childhood by the great Himalayan sage, Bengali Baba. Under the guidance of his master he traveled from monastery to monastery and studied with a variety of Himalayan saints and sages, including his grandmaster, who was living in a remote region of Tibet. In addition to this intense spiritual training, Swami Rama received higher education in both India and Europe. From 1949 to 1952, he held the prestigious position of Shankaracharya of Karvirpitham in South India. Thereafter, he returned to his master to receive further training at his cave monastery, and finally, in 1969, came to the United States, where he founded the Himalayan Institute. His best-known work, *Living with the Himalayan Masters*, reveals the many facets of this singular adept and demonstrates his embodiment of the living Himalayan Tradition.

# *the* Himalayan Institute

GLOBAL HEADQUARTERS (USA)

*The main building of the Himalayan Institute headquarters near Honesdale, Pennsylvania, USA.*

FOUNDED IN 1971 BY SWAMI RAMA, the Himalayan Institute has been dedicated to helping people grow physically, mentally, and spiritually by combining the best knowledge of both the East and the West.

Our international headquarters is located on a beautiful 400-acre campus in the rolling hills of the Pocono Mountains of northeastern Pennsylvania, USA. The atmosphere here is one to foster growth, increase inner awareness, and promote calm. Our grounds provide a wonderfully peaceful and healthy setting for our seminars and extended programs. Students from all over the world join us here to attend programs in such diverse areas as hatha yoga, meditation, stress reduction, ayurveda, nutrition, Eastern philosophy, psychology, and other subjects. Whether the programs are for weekend meditation retreats, week-long seminars on spirituality, months-long residential programs, or holistic health services, the attempt here is to provide an environment of gentle inner progress. We invite you to join with us in the ongoing process of personal growth and development.

# Programs and Services *include:*

The Institute is a nonprofit organization. Your membership in the Institute helps to support its programs. Please call or write for information on becoming a member.

Programs and Services Include:

- Himalayan Institute Press
- Seminars and Workshops
- Meditation Retreats
- Yoga Teacher Training
- Residential Programs
- Pancha Karma
- PureRejuv Wellness Center Products and Services
- Spiritual Excursions
- Humanitarian Projects and Community Centers in Africa, India and Mexico
- YogaInternational.com

For further information about our programs, humanitarian projects, and products,

**call:** +1 800-822-4547

**e-mail:** info@HimalayanInstitute.org

**write:** The Himalayan Institute
952 Bethany Turnpike
Honesdale, PA 18431

**or visit:** www.HimalayanInstitute.org

The Royal Path: Practical Lessons on Yoga ₹295
Wisdom of the Ancient Sages (Mundaka Upanishad) ₹295
Yoga and Psychotherapy ₹395

**Pandit Rajmani Tigunait, PhD**

From Death To Birth (Understanding Karma and Reincarnation) ₹295
Inner Quest: Yoga's Answers to Life's Questions ₹350
Lighting the Flame of Compassion ₹250
Sakti Sadhana (Tripura Rahasya) ₹350
Sakti: The Power in Tantra ₹350
Seven Systems of Indian Philosophy ₹350
Swami Rama of the Himalayas (Photobiography) ₹2500
Tantra Unveiled (Seducing the Forces of Matter and Spirit) ₹295
The Himalayan Masters: A Living Tradition ₹295
The Official Biography of Swami Rama of the Himalayas ₹395
The Power of Mantra & The Mystery of Initiation ₹295
The Pursuit of Power and Freedom: Katha Upanishad ₹295
The Secret of the Yoga Sutra: Samadhi Pada ₹695
Touched By Fire ₹395
Why We Fight ₹195

**Books by Other Authors**

Anatomy of Hatha Yoga, David Coulter PhD ₹695
Freedom From Stress, Phil Nuernberger, PhD ₹350
God, Swami Veda Bharati ₹295
Happiness: The Real Medicine, Blair Lewis ₹295
Healing the Whole Person, Swami Ajaya, PhD ₹295
Moving Inward: The Journey to Meditation, Rolf Sovik, PsyD ₹395
Philosophy of Hatha Yoga, Swami Veda Bharati ₹250
Spirit on the Move, Yoga International ₹295
The Muscle Book, Paul Blakey ₹250
The Practical Vedanta of Swami Rama Tirtha, Edited by Brandt Dayton ₹495
The Theory and Practice of Meditation, Rudolph Ballentine, M.D., Swami Rama ₹295
Yoga: Mastering the Basics (Photobook), Sandra Anderson & Rolf Sovik ₹995
Yoga Psychology (A Practical Guide to Meditation), Swami Ajaya, PhD ₹250
Yoga Sutras of Patanjali, Swami Veda Bharati ₹895

**Hindi Titles**

Anandmaya Jeevan Ka Utsav, Swami Rama ₹150
Himalaye ke Siddha Yogi: Sri Swami Rama (Shiksha aur Sadhana), Pandit Rajmani Tigunait ₹150
Himalaye ke Siddha Yogi: Sri Swami Rama (Yog Siddhi aur Vigyan), Pandit Rajmani Tigunait ₹150
Himalaye ke Santo ke Sang Niwas, Swami Rama ₹295
Ishopanishad, Swami Rama ₹95
Janam Mrithyu ka Rahasya (Kathopanishad), Swami Rama ₹125
Karam Bandhan se Mukti, Swami Rama ₹95